THE SOTADIC ZONE

This edition of THE SOTADIC ZONE is limited to two thousand and ten copies, ten copies of which are for the editors of THE PANURGE PRESS.

This volume is Number 751

THE SOTADIC ZONE

by

SIR RICHARD BURTON

PRIVATELY PRINTED BY
THE PANURGE PRESS
NEW YORK

CONTENTS

Preface, 9

The Sotadic Zone, 15

John A. Symonds' Criticism, 103

PREFACE

PREFACE

So many requests from professional men all over the country have reached us asking for this work or that published by the far-famed Kama Shastra Society of London and Benares[1] that we have decided to re-issue some of them in small, limited editions. The present volume is the first of these to make its appearance under the Panurge Press imprint.

It is hardly necessary to explain that Sir Richard Burton, the author of *The Sotadic Zone,* has done more than anyone else to draw aside the veil concealing the esoteric mysteries of sexuology. This curious and authoritative *livret* on pederasty appeared in his remarkable *Terminal Essay* to the original edition of the *Arabian Nights.*

---

[1] The Society brought out the following: Kama Sutra by Vatsyayana, 1883; Ananga Ranga by Kalyana Malla, 1885; The Arabian Nights by Burton, 1885-1886; The Perfumed Garden by Cheikh Nefzaoui, 1886; The Behâristan by Jami, 1887; The Gulistan by Sadi, 1888; The Nigaristan by Jawini (date unknown).

The publication of this Kama Shastra edition created a furor which shook the foundations of literary England, then at the crest of Victorian prudery. *The Sotadic Zone* was acidly attacked in press and pulpit by old women in crinolines and blue-nosed censors in petticoats.

Burton at the time defended himself in words which have long since passed into common currency: "To those critics who complain of my raw vulgarisms and puerile indecencies I can reply only by quoting what Dr. Johnson said to the lady who complained of the naughty words in his dictionary: 'You must have been looking for them, Madam!' "

But there is a justification deeper than any facetious reply. And Burton, to whom peace and quiet of character were total strangers, and who always carried chips on both shoulders, especially towards gratuitous advisers of "Thou shalt not's," justified his freedom of expression by the freedom of "the authors of the Authorized Version of the Bible, who did not hesitate to render *literatim* passages of a similar nature."[1]

---

[1] See page 100.

PREFACE

With characteristic contempt he declared: "To assert that such lore is unnecessary is to state, as every traveller knows, an *absurdum*. Few phenomena are more startling than the vision of a venerable infant, who has lived half his life in the midst of the wildest anthropological vagaries and monstrosities and yet who absolutely ignores all that India or Burmah enacts under his very eyes. This is crass ignorance, not the naive innocence of St. Francis who, seeing a man and a maid in a dark corner, raised his hands to Heaven and thanked the Lord that there was still in the world so much of Christian Charity."

Nevertheless, British Philistinism won the empty honors of the day and hour. *The Sotadic Zone* was deleted from the popular edition of Burton's *Arabian Nights*.

But time will not be robbed of its revenge. Burton's name today stands with the greatest names of the nineteenth century and all of the crew of kill-joy critics are buried in oblivion.

This edition of *The Sotadic Zone* is exactly as Burton wrote it. Nothing has been suppressed or expurgated.

We have appended a short criticism of it by John Addington Symonds, whose writings on Sexual Inversion have established him as an acknowledged authority on the subject.

THE PANURGE PRESS

THE SOTADIC ZONE
SIR RICHARD BURTON

THE SOTADIC ZONE

THE "execrabilis familia pathicorum" first came before me by a chance of earlier life. In 1845, when Sir Charles Napier had conquered and annexed Sind, despite a fraction (mostly venal) which sought favor with the now defunct "Court of Directors to the Honourable East India Company," the veteran began to consider his conquest with a curious eye. It was reported to him that Karáchi, a townlet of some two thousand souls and distant not more than a mile from camp, supported no less than three *lupanars*[1] or

---

[1] This detail especially excited the veteran's curiosity. The reason proved to be that the scrotum of the unmutilated boy could be used as a kind of bridle for directing the movements of the animal. I find nothing of the kind mentioned in the Sotadical literature of Greece and Rome; although the same cause might be expected everywhere to have the same effect. But in Mirabeau (Kadhésch) a *grand seigneur moderne,* when his *valet-de-chambre de confiance* proposes to provide him with women instead of boys, exclaims, "Des femmes! eh! c'est comme si tu me servais un gigot sans manche."

bordels, in which not women but boys and eunuchs, the former demanding nearly a double price, lay for hire. Being then the only British officer who could speak Sindi, I was asked indirectly to make enquiries and to report upon the subject; and I undertook the task on express condition that my report should not be forwarded to the Bombay Government, from whom supporters of the Conqueror's policy could expect scant favor, mercy or justice.

Accompanied by a Munshi, Mirza Mohammed Hosayn of Shiraz, and habited as a merchant, Mirza Abdullah the Bushiri[1] passed many an evening in the townlet, visited all the porneia and obtained the fullest details which were duly despatched to Government House.[2] But the "Devil's Brother" presently quitted Sind leaving in his

---

[1] See Falconry in the Valley of the Indus, London, John Van Voorst, 1852.

[2] Submitted to Government on Dec. 31, '47 and March 2, '48, they were printed in "Selections from the Records of the Government of India." Bombay. New Series. No. xvii. Part 2, 1855. These are (1) Notes on the Population of Sind, etc. and (2) Brief Notes on the Modes of Intoxication, etc. written in collaboration with my late friend, Assistant-Surgeon John E. Stocks, whose early death was a sore loss to scientific botany.

THE SOTADIC ZONE

office my unfortunate official: this found its way with sundry other reports to Bombay and produced the expected result. A friend in the Secretariat informed me that my summary dismissal from the service had been formally proposed by one of Sir Charles Napier's successors, whose decease compels me *parcere sepulto*. But this excess of outraged modesty was not allowed.

Subsequent enquiries in many and distant countries enabled me to arrive at the following conclusions:—

1. There exists what I shall call a "Sotadic Zone," bounded westwards by the northern shores of the Mediterranean (N. Lat. 43°) and by the southern (N. Lat. 30°). Thus the depth would be 780 to 800 miles including meridional France, the Iberian Peninsula, Italy and Greece, with the coast-regions of Africa from Morocco to Egypt.

2. Running eastward the Sotadic Zone narrows, embracing Asia Minor, Mesopotamia and Chaldæa, Afghanistan, Sind, the Punjab and Kashmir.

3. In Indo-China the belt begins to broaden, enfolding China, Japan and Turkistan.

4. It then embraces the South Sea Islands and the New World where, at the time of its discovery, Sotadic love was, with some exceptions, an established racial institution.

5. Within the Sotadic Zone the Vice is popular and endemic, held at the worst to be a mere peccadillo, whilst the races to the North and South of the limits here defined practise it only sporadically amid the opprobium of their fellows who, as a rule, are physically incapable of performing the operation and look upon it with the liveliest disgust.

Before entering into topographical details concerning Pederasty, which I hold to be geographical and climatic, not racial, I must offer a few considerations of its cause and origin.

We must not forget that the love of boys has its noble sentimental side. The Platonists and pupils of the Academy, followed by the Sufis or Moslem Gnostics, held such affection, pure as ardent, to be the *beau idéal* which united in man's soul the creature with the Creator. Professing to regard youths as the most cleanly and beautiful objects in this phenomenal world, they declared that by loving and extolling the *chef-d'œuvre,* corporeal and intellectual, of the Demiurgus, disinterestedly and without any admixture of carnal sensuality, they are paying the most fervent adoration to the *Causa causans*. They add that such affection, passing as it does the love of women, is far less selfish than fondness for and admiration of the other sex, which, however innocent, always suggest sexuality[1]; and Easterns add that the devotion of the moth to the taper is purer and more fervent than the Bulbul's love for the Rose.

Amongst the Greeks of the best ages the system of boy-favorites was advocated on considerations of morals and politics. The lover undertook the education of the beloved through precept and example, while the two were conjoined by a tie stricter than the fraternal. Hieronymus the Peripatetic strongly advocated it because the vigorous disposition of youths and the confidence

---

[1] Glycon the Courtesan in Athen. xiii. 84 declares that "boys are handsome only when they resemble women"; and so the Learned Lady in The Arabian Nights (vol. v, 160) declares "Boys are likened to girls because folks say, Yonder boy is like a girl." For the superior physical beauty of the human male compared with the female, see The Arabian Nights, vol. iv. 15; and the boy's voice before it breaks excels that of any diva.

engendered by their association often led to the overthrow of tyrannies. Socrates declared that "a most valiant army might be composed of boys and their lovers; for that of all men they would be most ashamed to desert one another." And even Virgil, despite the foul flavor of *Formosum pastor Corydon,* could write:—

<blockquote>Nisus amore pio pueri.</blockquote>

The only physical cause for the practice which suggests itself to me and that must be owned to be purely conjectural, is that within the Sotadic Zone there is a blending of the masculine and feminine temperaments, a crasis which elsewhere occurs only sporadically. Hence the male *féminisme* whereby the man becomes *patiens* as well as *agens,* and the woman a tribade, a votary of mascula Sappho,[1] Queen of Frictrices or Rubbers.[2]

---

[1] "Mascula," from the priapiscus, the over-development of clitoris (the veretrum muliebre, in Arabic Abu Tartúr, habens cristam) which enabled her to play the man. Sappho (nat. B.C. 612) has been *retoillée* like Mary Stuart, La Brinvilliers, Marie Antoinette and a host of feminine names which have a savor not of sanctity. Maximus of Tyre (Dissert. xxiv.) declares that the Eros of Sappho was Socratic and that Gyrinna and Atthis were as Alcibiades and Chermides to Socrates: Ovid, who could con-

THE SOTADIC ZONE 〜 〜 〜 21

Professor Mantegazza claims to have discovered the cause of this pathological love, this perversion of the erotic sense, one of the marvellous list of amorous vagaries which deserve, not prosecution but the pitiful care of the physician and the study of the psychologist. According to him the nerves of the rectum and the genitalia, in all

---

sult documents now lost, takes the same view in the Letter of Sappho to Phaon and in Tristia ii. 265.
        Lesbia quid docuit Sappho nisi amare puellas?
Suidas supports Ovid. Longinus eulogizes the ἐρωτική μανία (a term applied only to carnal love) of the far-famed Ode to Atthis:—

    Ille mî par esse Deo videtur . . .
    (Heureux! qui près de toi pour toi seule soupire . . .
    Blest as th' immortal gods is he, etc.)

By its love symptoms, suggesting that possession is the sole cure for passion, Erasistratus discovered the love of Antiochus for Stratonice. Mure (Hist. of Greek Literature, 1850) speaks of the Ode to Aphrodite (Frag. 1) as "one in which the whole volume of Greek literature offers the most powerful concentration into one brilliant focus of the modes in which amatory concupiscence can display itself." But Bernhardy, Bode, Richter, K. O. Müller and especially Welcker have made Sappho a model of purity, much like some of our dull wits who have converted Shakespeare, that most debauched genius, into a good British bourgeois.

[2] The Arabic Sahhákah, the Tractatrix or Subigitatrix. Hence to Lesbianise (λεσβίζειν) and tribassare (τρίβεσθαι); the former applied to the love of woman for woman and the latter to its

cases closely connected, are abnormally so in the pathic who obtains, by intromission, the venereal orgasm which is usually sought through the sexual organs. So amongst women there are tribads who can procure no pleasure except by foreign objects introduced *a posteriori*. Hence his threefold distribution of sodomy; (1) Peripheric or anatomical, caused by an unusual distribution of the nerves and their hyperæsthesia; (2) Luxurious, when love *a tergo* is preferred on account of the narrowness of the passage; and (3) the Psychical. But this is evidently superficial; the question is what causes this neuropathy, this abnormal distribution and condition of the nerves.[1]

---

mécanique: this is either natural, as friction of the labia and insertion of the clitoris when unusually developed; or artificial by means of the fascinum, the artificial penis (the Persian "Mayájang"); the *patte de chat*, the banana-fruit and a multitude of other *succedanea*. As this feminine perversion is only glanced at in The Arabian Nights I need hardly enlarge upon the subject.

[1] Plato (Symp.) is probably mystical when he accounts for such passions by there being in the beginning three species of humanity, men, women and men-women or androgynes. When the latter were destroyed by Zeus for rebellion, the two others were individually divided into equal parts. Hence each division seeks its other half in the same sex; the primitive man prefers men and the primitive woman women. *C'est beau*, but—is it true?

THE SOTADIC ZONE ᴗ ᴗ ᴗ 23

As Prince Bismarck finds a moral difference between the male and female races of history, so I suspect a mixed physical temperament effected by the manifold subtle influences massed together in the word climate. Something of the kind is necessary to explain the fact of this pathological love extending over the greater portion of the habitable world, without any apparent connection of race or media, from the polished Greek to the cannibal Tupi of the Brazil.

Walt Whitman speaks of the ashen grey faces of onanists: the faded colors, the puffy features and the unwholesome complexion of the pro-

---

The idea was probably derived from Egypt, which supplied the Hebrews with androgynic humanity; and thence it passed to extreme India, where Shiva as Ardhanári was male on one side and female on the other side of the body, combining paternal and maternal qualities and functions. The first creation of humans (Gen. i. 27) was hermaphrodite (= Hermes and Venus) *masculum et fœminam creavit eos*—male and female created He them—on the sixth day, with the command to increase and multiply (ibid. v. 28) while Eve the woman was created subsequently. Meanwhile, say certain Talmudists, Adam carnally copulated with all races of animals. See L'Anandryne in Mirabeau's Erotika Biblion, where Antoinette Bourgnon laments the undoubling which disfigured the work of God, producing monsters incapable of independent self-reproduction like the vegetable kingdom.

fessed pederast with his peculiar cachetic expression, indescribable but once seen never forgotten, stamp the breed, and Doctor Adolph is justified in declaring "Alle Gewohnheits-paederasten erkennen sich einander schnell, oft mit einen Blick." This has nothing in common with the *féminisme* which betrays itself in the pathic by womanly gait, regard and gesture: it is a something *sui generis;* and the same may be said of the color and look of the young priest who honestly refrains from women and their substitutes.

Doctor Tardieu, in his well-known work, "Etude medico-légale sur les Attentats aux Mœurs," and Doctor Adolph note a peculiar infundibuliform disposition of the "After" and a smoothness and want of folds even before any abuse has taken place, together with special forms of the male organs in confirmed pederasts. But these observations have been rejected by Caspar, Hoffman, Brouardel and Doctor Henry Coutagne,[1] and it is a medical question whose discussion would here be out of place.

The origin of pederasty is lost in the night of ages; but its *historique* has been carefully traced

---

[1] Notes sur la Sodomie, Lyon, 1880.

THE SOTADIC ZONE 〜 〜 〜 25

by many writers, especially Virey,[1] Rosenbaum[2] and Meier.[3] The ancient Greeks who, like the modern Germans, invented nothing but were great improvers of what other races invented, attributed the formal apostolate of Sotadism to Orpheus, whose stigmata were worn by the Thracian women;

> —Omnemque refugerat Orpheus
> Fœmineam venerem;—
> Ille etiam Thracum populis fuit auctor, amorem
> In teneres transferre mares: citraque juventam
> Ætatis breve ver, et primos carpere flores.
> Ovid Met. x. 79-85.

Euripides proposed Laïus, father of Oedipus, as the inaugurator, whereas Timæus declared that the fashion of making favorites of boys was introduced into Greece from Crete, for Malthusian reasons said Aristotle (Pol. ii. 10) attribut-

---

[1] De la Femme, Paris, 1827.

[2] Die Lustseuche des Alterthum's, Halle, 1839.

[3] See his exhaustive article on (Grecian) "Paederastie" in the Allgemeine Encyclopædie of Ersch and Gruber, Leipzig, Brockhaus, 1837. He carefully traces it through the several states, Dorians, Æolians, Ionians, the Attic cities and those of Asia Minor. For these details I must refer my readers to M. Meier; a full account of these would fill a volume.

ing it to Minos. Herodotus, however, knew far better, having discovered (ii. c. 80) that the Orphic and Bacchic rites were originally Egyptian. But the Father of History was a traveller and an annalist rather than an archæologist and he tripped in the following passage (i. c. 135), "As soon as the Persians hear of any luxury, they instantly make it their own, and hence, among other matters, they have learned from the Hellenes a passion for boys" ("unnatural lust," says the very modest Rawlinson). Plutarch (De Malig, Herod, xiii.)[1] asserts with much more probability that the Persians used eunuch boys according to the *Mos Græciæ,* long before they had seen the Grecian main.

In the Holy Books of the Hellenes, Homer and Hesiod, dealing with the heroic ages, there is no trace of pederasty, although, in a long subsequent generation, Lucian suspected Achilles and Patroclus as he did Orestes and Plyades, Theseus and Pirithous. Homer's praises of beauty are reserved for the feminines, especially his favorite Helen.

---

[1] Against which see Henri Estienne, Apologie pour Hérodote, a society satire of the sixteenth century, reprinted by Liseux.

But the Dorians of Crete seem to have commended the abuse to Athens and Sparta and subsequently imported it into Tarentum, Agrigentum and other colonies. Ephorus in Strabo (x. 4 § 21) gives a curious account of the violent abduction of beloved boys by the lover; of the obligations of the ravisher to the favorite[1] and of the marriage-ceremonies which continued for two months. See also Plato Laws i. c. 8. Servius (Ad Æneid. x. 325) informs us "De Cretensibus accepimus, quod in amore puerorum intemperantes fuerunt, quod postea in Laconas et in totam Græciam translatum est." The Cretans and afterwards their apt pupils the Chalcidians held it disreputable for a beautiful boy to lack a lover. Hence Zeus, the national Doric god of Crete, loved Ganymede[2]; Apollo, another Dorian deity,

---

[1] In Sparta the lover was called εἰσπνήλας and the beloved as in Thessaly ἀίτης.

[2] The more I study religions the more I am convinced that man never worshipped anything but himself. Zeus, who became Jupiter, was an ancient king, according to the Cretans, who were entitled liars because they showed his burial-place. From a deified ancestor he would become a local god, like the Hebrew Jehovah as opposed to Chemosh of Moab; the name would gain amplitude by long time and distant travel and the old island chieftain would end in becoming the Demiurgus. Ganymede

loved Hyacinth; and Hercules, a Doric hero who grew to be a sun-god, loved Hylas and a host of others: thus Crete sanctified the practice by the examples of the gods and demigods.

But when legislation came, the subject had qualified itself for legal limitation and as such was undertaken by Lycurgus and Solon, according to Xenophon (Lac. ii. 13), who draws a broad distinction between the honest love of boys and dishonest (αἴχιστος) lust. They both approved of pure pederastia, like that of Harmodius and Aristogiton; but forbade it with serviles because degrading to a free man. Hence the love of boys was spoken of like that of women, (Plato: Phædrus; Repub. vi. c. 19 and Xenophon, Synop. iv. 10) *e.g.*, "There was once a boy, or rather a youth, of exceeding beauty and he had very many lovers"—this is the language of Hafiz and Sa'adi.

(who possibly gave rise to the old Lat. "Catamitus") was probably some fair Phrygian boy ("son of Tros") who in process of time became a symbol of the wise man seized by the eagle (perspicacity) to be raised amongst the Immortals; and the chaste myth simply signified that only the prudent are loved by the gods. But it rotted with age as do all things human. For the Pederastia of the Gods see Bayle under Chrysippe.

Æschylus, Sophocles and Euripides were allowed to introduce it upon the stage, for "many men were as fond of having boys for their favorites as women for their mistresses; and this was a frequent fashion in many well-regulated cities of Greece." Poets like Alcæus, Anacreon, Agathon and Pindar affected it and Theognis sang of "a beautiful boy in the flower of his youth." The statesmen Aristides and Themistocles quarreled over Stesileus of Teos; and Pisistratus loved Charmus who first built an altar to Puerile Eros, while Charmus loved Hippias, son of Pisistratus.

Demosthenes the Orator took into keeping a youth called Cnosion greatly to the indignation of his wife. Xenophon loved Clinias and Autolycus; Aristotle, Hermeas, Theodectes[1] and others; Empedocles, Pausanias; Epicurus, Pytocles; Aristippus, Eutichydes and Zeno with his Stoics had a philosophic disregard for women, affecting only pederastia. A man in Athenæus

---

[1] See Dissertation sur les idées morales des Grecs et sur les danger de lire Platon. Par M. Audé, Bibliophile, Rouen, Lemonnyer, 1879. This is the pseudonym of the late Octave Delepierre, who published with Gay, but not the Editio Princeps—which, if I remember rightly, contains much more matter.

(iv. c. 40) left in his will that certain youths he had loved should fight like gladiators at his funeral; and Charicles in Lucian abuses Callicratidas for his love of "sterile pleasures."

Lastly there was the notable affair of Alcibiades and Socrates, the "sanctus pæderasta"[1] being *violemment soupçonné* when under the mantle:—*non semper sine plagâ ab eo surrexit.* Athenæus (v. c. 13) declares that Plato represents Socrates as absolutely intoxicated with his passion for Alcibiades.[2] The ancients seem to

---

[1] The phrase of J. Matthias Gesner, Comm. Reg. Soc. Gottingen i. 1-32. It was founded upon Erasmus' "Sancte Socrate, ora pro nobis," and the article was translated by M. Alcide Bonneau, Paris, Liseux, 1877.

[2] The subject has employed many a pen, *e. g.* Alcibiade Fanciullo a Scola, D. P. A. (supposed to be Pietro Aretino—*ad captandum?*), Oranges, par Juann Wart, 1652: small square 8vo. of pp. 102, including 3 preliminary pp. and at end an unpaged leaf with 4 sonnets, almost Venetian, by V. M. There is a re-impression of the same date, a small 12mo of longer format, pp. 124 with pp. 2 for sonnets: in 1862 the Imprimerie Raçon printed 102 copies in 8 vo. of pp. iv.-108, and in 1863 it was condemned by the police as a *liber spurcissimus atque execrandus de criminis sodomici laude et arte.* This work produced "Alcibiade Enfant à l'école," traduit pour la première fois de l'Italien de Ferrante Pallavicini, Amsterdam, chez l'Ancien Pierre Marteau, mdccclxvi. Pallavicini (nat. 1618), who wrote against

have held the connection impure, or Juvenal would not have written—

Inter Socraticos notissima fossa cinædos,

followed by Firmicus (vii. 14) who speaks of "Socratici pædicones." It is the modern fashion to doubt the pederasty of the master of Hellenic Sophrosyne, the "Christian before Christianity"; but such a world-wide term as Socratic love can hardly be explained by the *lucus-a-non-lucendo* theory. We are overapt to apply our nineteenth

---

Rome, was beheaded, æt. 26 (March 5, 1644) at Avignon in 1644 by the vengeance of the Barberini: he was a *bel esprit déréglé, nourri d'études antiques* and a member of the Acad. Degl' Incogniti. His peculiarities are shown by his "Opere Scelte," 2 vols. 12mo, Villafranca, mdclxiii.; these do not include Alcibiade Fanciullo, a dialogue between Philotimus and Alcibiades which seems to be a mere skit at the Jesuits and their *Péché philosophique*. Then came the "Dissertation sur l'Alcibiade fanciullo a scola," traduit de l'Italien de Giambattista Baseggio et accompagnée de notes et d'une post-face par un bibliophile français (M. Gustave Brunet, Librarian of Bordeaux), Paris. J. Gay, 1861—an octavo of pp. 78 (paged), 254 copies. The same Baseggio printed in 1850 his Disquisizioni (23 copies) and claims for F. Pallavicini the authorship of Alcibiades which the Manuel du Libraire wrongly attributes to M. Girol. Adda in 1859. I have heard of but not seen the "Amator fornaceus, amator ineptus" (Palladii, 1633) supposed by some to be the origin of Alcibiade Fanciullo; but most critics consider it a poor and insipid production.

century prejudices and prepossessions to the morality of the ancient Greeks who would have specimen'd such squeamishness in Attic salt.

The Spartans, according to Agnon the Academic (confirmed by Plato, Plutarch and Cicero), treated boys and girls in the same way before marriage: hence Juvenal (xi. 173) uses "Lacedæmonius" for a pathic and other writers apply it to a tribade. After the Peloponnesian War, which ended in B.C. 404, the use became merged in the abuse. Yet some purity must have survived, even amongst the Bœotians who produced the famous Narcissus,[1] described by Ovid (Met. iii. 339):—

> Multi illum juvenes, multæ cupiere puellæ;
> Nulli illum juvenes, nullæ tetigere puellæ:[2]

---

[1] The word is from νάρκη, numbness, torpor, narcotism: the flowers, being loved by the infernal gods, were offered to the Furies. Narcissus and Hippolytus are often assumed as types of *morosa voluptas,* masturbation and clitorization for nymphomania: certain mediæval writers found in the former a type of the Savior; and Mirabeau a representation of the androgynous or first Adam: to me Narcissus suggests the Hindu Vishnu absorbed in the contemplation of his own perfections.

[2] The verse of Ovid is parallel'd by the song of Al-Záhir al-Jazari (Ibn Khall. iii. 720).

> Illum impuberem amaverunt mares; puberem feminæ.
> Gloria Deo! nunquam amatoribus carebit.

THE SOTADIC ZONE 33

for Epaminondas, whose name is mentioned with three beloveds, established the Holy Regiment composed of mutual lovers, testifying the majesty of Eros and preferring to a discreditable life a glorious death. Philip's reflections on the fatal field of Chaeroneia form their fittest epitaph. At last the Athenians, according to Æschines, officially punished Sodomy with death; but the threat did not abolish *bordels* of boys, like those of Karáchi; the Porneia and Pornoboskeia, where slaves and *pueri venales* "stood," as the term was, near the Pnyx, the city walls and a certain tower, also about Lycabettus (Æsch. contra Tim.); and paid a fixed tax to the state. The pleasures of society in civilized Greece seem to have been sought chiefly in the heresies of love—Hetairesis[1] and Sotadism.

---

[1] The venerable society of prostitutes contained three chief classes. The first and lowest were the Dicteriads, so called from Diete (Crete) who imitated Pasiphaë, wife of Minos, in preferring a bull to a husband; above them was the middle class, the Aleutridæ who were the Almahs or professional musicians, and the aristocracy was represented by the Hetairai, whose wit and learning enabled them to adorn more than one page of Grecian history. The grave Solon, who had studied in Egypt, established a vast Dicterion (Philemon in his Delphica), or *bordel*, whose proceeds swelled the revenue of the Republic.

It is calculated that the French of the sixteenth century had four hundred names for the parts genital and three hundred for their use in coition. The Greek vocabulary is not less copious and some of its pederastic terms, of which Meier gives nearly a hundred, and its nomenclature of pathologic love are curious and picturesque enough to merit quotation.

To live the life of Abron (the Argive), *i.e.* that of a πάσχων, pathic or passive lover.

The Agathonian song.

Aischrourgía = dishonest love, also called Akolasía, Akrasía, Arrenokoitía, etc.

Alcinoan youths, or "non-conformists,"

<blockquote>In cute curandâ plus æquo operata Juventus.</blockquote>

Alegomenos, the "unspeakable," as the pederast was termed by the Council of Ancyra: also the Agrios, Apolaustus and Akolastos.

Androgyne, of whom Ansonius wrote (Epig. lxviii. 15):—

<blockquote>Ecce ego sum factus femina de puero.</blockquote>

Badas and Badízein = clunes torquens: also Bátalos = a catamite.

THE SOTADIC ZONE 35

Catapygos, Katapygosyne = puerarius and catadactylium from Dactylion, the ring, used in the sense of Nerissa's, but applied to the *corollarium puerile*.

Cinædus (Kínaidos), the active lover (ποιών) derived either from his kinetics or quasi κύων αἴδως = dog-modest. Also Spatalocinædus (lasciviâ fluens) = a fair Ganymede.

Chalcidissare (Khalkidizein), from Chalcis in Eubœa, a city famed for love *à posteriori*; mostly applied to *le léchement des testicules* by children.

Clazomenæ = the buttocks, also a sotadic disease, so called from the Ionian city devoted to Aversa Venus; also used of a pathic,
—et tergo femina pube vir est.

Embasicoetas, properly a link-boy at marriages, also a "night-cap" drunk before bed and lastly an effeminate; one who *perambulavit omnium cubilia* (Catullus). See Encolpius' pun upon the Embasicoetas in Satyricon, cap. iv.

Epipedesis, the carnal assault.

Geiton, literally "neighbor," the beloved of Encolpius, which has produced the French Giton = Bardache, Italian Bardascia from the Arabic

Baradaj, a captive, a slave; the augmented form is Polygeiton.

Hippias (tyranny of), employed when the patient (woman or boy) mounts the agent. Aristophenes Vesp. 502. So also Kelitizein = *peccare superne* or *equum agitare supernum* of Horace.

Mokhthería, depravity with boys.

Paidika, whence *pædicare* (active) and *pædicari* (passive): so in the Latin poet:—

> PEnelopes primam DIdonis prima sequatur,
> Et primam CAni, syllaba prima REmi.

Pathikos, Pathicus, a passive, like Malakos (malacus, mollis, facilis), Malchio, Trimalchio (Petronius), Malta, Maltha and in Horace (Sat. ii. 25)

> Malthinus tunicis demissis ambulat.

Praxis = the malpractice.

Pygisma = buttockry, because most actives end within the nates, being too much excited for further intromission.

Phœnicissare (φοινικίζειν)=*cunnilingere in tempore menstruum, quia hoc vitium in Phœnicia generata solebat;* also *irrumer en miel*.

Phicidissare, denotat actum per canes commissum quando *lambunt cunnos vel testiculos* (Suetonius): also applied to pollution of childhood.

Samorium flores (Erasmus, Prov. xxiii.), alluding to the androgynic prostitutions of Samos.

Siphniassare (σιφνιάζειν, from Siphnos, hod. Sifanto Island)=*digito podicem fodere ad pruriginem restinguendam,* says Erasmus (see Mirabeau's Erotika Biblion, Anoscopie).

Thrypsis = the rubbing.

Pederastia had in Greece, I have shown, its noble and ideal side: Rome, however, borrowed her malpractices, like her religion and polity, from those ultra-material Etruscans and debauched with a brazen face. Even under the Republic Plautus (Casin. ii. 21) makes one of his characters exclaim, in the utmost *sang-froid,* "Ultro te, amator, apage te a dorso meo!" With increased luxury the evil grew and Livy notices (xxxix. 13), at the Bacchanalia, *plura virorum inter sese quam fœminarum stupra.*

There were individual protests; for instance, S. Q. Fabius Maximus Servilianus (Consul U.C. 612) punished his son for *dubia castitas;* and a private soldier, C. Plotius, killed his military Tribune, Q. Luscius, for unchaste proposals. The

Lex Scantinia (Scatinia?), popularly derived from Scantinius the Tribune and of doubtful date (B.C. 226?), attempted to abate the scandal by fine and the Lex Julia by death; but they were trifling obstacles to the flood of infamy which surged in with the Empire.

No class seems then to have disdained these "sterile pleasures": "l'on n'attachoit point alors à cette espéce d'amour une note d'infamie, comme en païs de chrétienté," says Bayle under "Anacreon." The great Cæsar, the *Cinædus calvus* of Catallus, was the husband of all the wives and the wife of all the husbands in Rome (Suetonius, cap. lii.); and his soldiers sang in his praise *Gallias Cæsar subegit, Nicomedes Cæsarem* (Suet. cies. xlix.); whence his sobriquet "Fornix Birthynicus." Of Augustus the people chanted

Videsne ut Cinædus orbem digito temperet?

Tiberius, with his *pisciculi and greges exoletorum,* invented the *Symplegma* or *nexus* of Sellarii, *agentes et patientes,* in which the spinthriæ (literally women's bracelets) were connected in a chain by the bond of flesh[1] (Seneca Quæst.

---

[1] This and Saint Paul (Romans i. 27) suggested to Caravag-

THE SOTADIC ZONE 39

Nat.). Of this refinement, which in the earlier part of the nineteenth century was renewed by sundry Englishmen at Naples, Ausonius wrote (Epig. cxix. 1),

> Tres uno in lecto: stuprum duo perpetiuntur;

And Martial had said (xii. 43)

> Quo symplegmate quinque copulentur;
> Qua plures teneantur a catena; etc.

Ausonius recounts of Caligula he so lost patience that he forcibly entered the priest M. Lepidus, before the sacrifice was completed. The beautiful Nero was formally married to Pythagoras (or Doryphoros) and afterwards took to wife Sporus who was first subjected to castration of a peculiar fashion; he was then named Sabina, after the deceased spouse and claimed queenly honors. The "Othonis et Trajani pathici" were famed; the great Hadrian openly loved Antinoüs and the wild debaucheries of Heliogabalus seem only to have amused, instead of disgusting, the Romans.

Uranopolis allowed public *lupanaria* where adults and *meritorii pueri,* who began their career

---

gio his picture of St. Rosario (in the museum of the Grand Duke of Tuscany), showing a circle of thirty men *turpiter ligati.*

as early as seven years, stood for hire: the inmates of these *cauponæ* wore sleeved tunics and dalmatics like women. As in modern Egypt pathic boys, we learn from Catullus, haunted the public baths. Debauchees had signals like freemasons whereby they recognized one another. The Greek Skematízein was made by closing the hand to represent the scrotum and raising the middle finger as if to feel whether a hen had eggs, *tâter si les poulettes ont l'œuf*: hence the Athenians called it Catapygon or sodomite and the Romans *digitus impudicus* or *infamis,* the "medical finger[1]" of Rabelais and the Chiromantists. Another sign was to scratch the head with the minimus—*digitulo caput scabere* (Juv. ix. 133).[2]

The prostitution of boys was first forbidden by Domitian; but Saint Paul, a Greek, had formally expressed his abomination of the Vice

---

[1] Properly speaking "Medicus" is the third or ring-finger, as shown by the old Chiromantist verses,

> Est pollex Veneris; sed Jupiter indice gaudet
> Saturnus medium; Sol *medicum*que tenet.

[2] So Seneca uses *digito scalpit caput.* The modern Italian does the same by inserting the thumb-tip between the index and medius to suggest the clitoris.

THE SOTADIC ZONE ⌣ ⌣ ⌣ 41

(Rom. i. 26; i. Cor. vi. 8); and we may agree with Grotius (de Verit. ii. c. 13) that early Christianity did much to suppress it. At last the Emperor Theodosius punished it with fire as a profanation, because *sacrosanctum esse debetur hospitium virilis animæ.*

In the pagan days of imperial Rome her literature makes no difference between boy and girl. Horace naïvely says (Sat. ii. 118):—

<blockquote>Ancilla aut verna est præsto puer;</blockquote>

and with Hamlet, but in a dishonest sense:—

<blockquote>—Man delights me not
Nor woman neither.</blockquote>

Similarly the Spaniard Martial, who is a mine of such pederastic allusions (xi. 46):—

<blockquote>Sive puer arrisit, sive puella tibi.</blockquote>

That marvellous Satyricon which unites the wit of Molière [1] with the debaucheries of Piron,

---

[1] What can be wittier than the now trite Tale of the Ephesian Matron, whose dry humor is worthy of The Arabian Nights? No wonder that it has made the grand tour of the world. It is found in the neo-Phædrus, the tales of Musæus and in the Septem Sapientes as the "Widow which was comforted." As the "Fabliau de la Femme qui se fist putain sur la fosse de son Mari," it tempted Brantôme and La Fontaine; and Abel Rému-

whilst the writer has been described, like Rabelais, as *purissimus in impuritate,* is a kind of Triumph of Pederasty. Geiton the hero, a handsome curly-pated hobbledehoy of seventeen, with his *câlinerie* and wheedling tongue, is courted like one of the *sequior sexus*: his lovers are inordinately jealous of him and his desertion leaves deep scars upon the heart. But no dialogue between man and wife *in extremis* could be more pathetic than that in the scene where shipwreck is imminent. Elsewhere every one seems to attempt his neighbor: a man *alte succinctus* assails Ascyltos; Lycus, the Tarentine skipper, would force Encolpius, and so forth: yet we have the neat finished touch (cap. vii.):—"The lamentation was very fine (the dying man having manumitted his slaves) albeit his wife wept not as though she loved him. *How were it, had he not behaved to her so well?*"

---

sat shows in his Contes Chinois that it is well known to the Middle Kingdom. Walter K. Kelly remarks, that the most singular place for such a tale is the "Rule and Exercise of Holy Dying" by Jeremy Taylor, who introduces it into his chapt. v.—"Of the Contingencies of Death and Treating our Dead." But in those days divines were not mealy-mouthed.

THE SOTADIC ZONE 43

Erotic Latin glossaries[1] give some ninety words connected with Pederasty and some, which "speak with Roman simplicity," are peculiarly expressive. "Aversa Venus" alludes to women being treated as boys: hence Martial, translated by Piron, addresses Mistress Martial (x.44):—

> Teque puta, cunnos, uxor, habere duos.

The *capillatus* or *comatus* is also called *calamistratus*, the darling curled with crisping-irons; and he is an Effeminatus, *i.e. qui muliebria patitur*; or a Delicatus, slave or eunuch for the use of the Draucus, Puerarius (boy-lover) or Dominus (Mart. xi. 71). The Divisor is so called from his practice, *Hillas dividere* or *cædere,* something like Martial's *cacare mentulam* or Juvenal's *Hes-*

---

[1] Glossarium eroticum linguæ Latinæ, sive theogoniæ, legum et morum nuptialium apud Romanos explanatio nova, auctore P. P. (Parisiis, Dondey-Dupré, 1826, in 8vo). P. P. is supposed to be Chevalier Pierre Pierrugues, an engineer who made a plan of Bordeaux and who annotated the Erotica Biblion. Gay writes, "On s'est servi pour cet ouvrage des travaux inédits de M. le Baron de Schonen, etc. Quant au Chevalier Pierre Pierrugues, qu'on désignait comme l'auteur de ce savant volume, son existence n'est pas bien avérée, et quelques bibliographies persistent à penser que ce nom cache la collaboration du Baron de Schonen et d'Eloi Johanneau." Other glossicists as Blondeau and Forberg have been printed by Liseux, Paris.

ternæ occurrere cænæ. Facere vicibus (Juv. vii. 238), *incestare se invicem or mutuum facere* (Plaut. Trin. ii. 437), is described as "a puerile vice," in which the two take turns to be active and passive: they are also called Gemelli and Fratres = *compares in pædicatione. Illicita libido is* = *præpostera seu postica Venus,* and is expressed by the picturesque phrase *indicare (seu incurvare) aliquem. Depilatus, divellere pilos, glaber, lævis* and *nates pervellere* are allusions to the Sotadic toilette. The fine distinction between *demittere* and *dejicere caput* are worthy of a glossary, while *Pathica puella, puera, putus, pullipremo, pusio, pygiaca sacra, quadrupes, scarabæus* and *smerdalius* explain themselves.

From Rome the practice extended far and wide to her colonies, especially the Provincia now called Provence. Athenæus (xii. 26) charges the people of Massilia with "acting like women out of luxury"; and he cites the saying "May you sail to Massilia!" as if it were another Corinth. Indeed the whole Keltic race is charged with the Vice by Aristotle (Pol. ii. 66), Strabo. (iv. 199) and Diodorus Siculus (v. 32). Roman civilization carried pederasty also to Northern Africa,

THE SOTADIC ZONE 45

where it took firm root, while the negro and negroid races to the South ignore the erotic perversion, except where imported by foreigners into such kingdoms as Bornu and Haussa. In old Mauritania, now Morocco,[1] the Moors proper are notable sodomites; Moslems, even of saintly houses, are permitted openly to keep catamites, nor do their disciples think worse of their sanctity for such license: in one case the English wife failed to banish from the home "that horrid boy."

Yet pederasty is forbidden by the Koran. In chapter iv. 20, we read; "And if two (men)

---

[1] This magnificent country which the petty jealousies of Europe condemn, like the glorious regions about Constantinople, to mere barbarism, is tenanted by three Moslem races. The Berbers, who call themselves Tamazight (plural of Amazigh), are the Gætulian indigenes speaking an Africo-Semitic tongue (see Essai de Grammaire Kabyle, etc. par A. Hanoteau, Paris, Benjamin Duprat). The Arabs, descended from the conquerors in our eighth century, are mostly nomads and camel-breeders. Third and last are the Moors proper, the race dwelling in towns, a mixed breed originally Arabian but modified by six centuries of Spanish residence and showing by thickness of feature and a parchment-colored skin, resembling the American Octaroons, a negro innervation of old date. The latter are well described in "Morocco and the Moors," etc. (Sampson Low and Co., 1876), by my late friend, Dr. Arthur Leared, whose work I should like to see reprinted.

among you commit the crime, then punish them both," the penalty being some hurt or damage by public reproach, insult or scourging.

There are four distinct references to Lot and the Sodomites in chapters vii. 78; xi. 77-84; xxvi. 160-174 and xxix. 28-35. In the first the prophet commissioned to the people says, "Proceed ye to a fulsome act wherein no creature hath foregone ye? Verily ye come to men in lieu of women lustfully." We have then an account of the rain which made an end of the wicked and this judgment on the Cities of the Plain is repeated with more detail in the second reference. Here the angels, generally supposed to be three, Gabriel, Michael and Raphael, appeared to Lot as beautiful youths, a sore temptation to the sinners and the godly man's arm was straightened concerning his visitors because he felt unable to protect them from the erotic vagaries of his fellow townsmen. He therefore shut his doors and from behind them argued the matter: presently the riotous assembly attempted to climb the wall when Gabriel, seeing the distress of his host, smote them on the face with one of his wings and blinded them so that all moved off crying for aid

THE SOTADIC ZONE 47

and saying that Lot had magicians in his house.

Hereupon the "cities" which, if they ever existed, must have been Fellah villages, were uplifted: Gabriel thrust his wing under them and raised them so high that the inhabitants of the lower heaven (the lunar sphere) could hear the dogs barking and the cocks crowing. Then came the rain of stones: these were clay pellets baked in hell-fire, streaked white and red, or having some mark to distinguish them from the ordinary, and each bearing the name of its destination like the missiles which destroyed the host of Abrahat al-Ashram.[1] Lastly the "cities" were turned upside down and cast upon earth.

These circumstantial unfacts are repeated at full length in the other two chapters; but rather as an instance of Allah's power than as a warning against pederasty, which Mohammed seems to have regarded with philosophic indifference. The general opinion of his followers is that it should be punished like fornication unless the of-

---

[1] Thus somewhat agreeing with one of the multitudinous modern theories that the Pentapolis was destroyed by discharges of meteoric stones during a tremendous thunderstorm. Possible, but where are the stones?

fenders made a public act of penitence. But here, as in adultery, the law is somewhat too clement and will not convict unless four credible witnesses swear to have seen *rem in re*. I have noticed (vol. i. 211) the vicious opinion that the Ghilmán or Wuldán, the beautiful boys of Paradise, the counterparts of the Houris, will be lawful catamites to the True Believers in a future state of happiness: the idea is nowhere countenanced in Al-Islam; and, although I have often heard debauchees refer to it, the learned look upon the assertion as scandalous.

As in Morocco, so the Vice prevails throughout the old regencies of Algiers, Tunis and Tripoli and all the cities of the South Mediterranean seaboard, whilst it is unknown to the Nubians, the Berbers and the wilder tribes dwelling inland. Proceeding Eastward we reach Egypt, that classical region of all abominations which, marvellous to relate, flourished in closest contact with men leading the purest of lives, models of moderation and morality, of religion and virtue. Amongst the ancient Copts the Vice was part and portion of the Ritual and was represented by two male partridges alternately copulating (Interp. in

Priapi Carm. xvii). The evil would have gained strength by the invasion of Cambyses (B.C. 524), whose armies, after the victory over Psammenitus, settled in the Nile Valley, and held it, despite sundry revolts, for some hundred and ninety years. During these six generations the Iranians left their mark upon Lower Egypt and especially, as the late Rogers Bey proved, upon the Fayyum the most ancient Delta of the Nile.[1] Nor would the evil be diminished by the Hellenes who, under Alexander the Great, "liberator and savior of Egypt" (B.C. 332), extinguished the native dynasties: the love of the Macedonian for Bagoas the Eunuch being a matter of history.

From that time and under the rule of the Ptolemies the morality gradually decayed; the Canopic orgies extended into private life and the debauchery of the men was equalled only by the depravity of the women. Neither Christianity nor Al-Islam could effect a change for the better;

---

[1] To this Iranian domination I attribute the use of many Persic words which are not yet obsolete in Egypt. "Bakhshish," for instance, is not intelligible in the Moslem regions west of the Nile Valley, and for a present the Moors say Hadiyah, *regalo* or favor.

and social morality seems to have been at its worst during the past century when Sonnini travelled (A.D. 1717). The French officer, who is thoroughly trustworthy, draws the darkest picture of the widely-spread criminality especially of the bestiality and the sodomy (chapt. xv.) which formed the "delight of the Egyptians." During the Napoleonic conquest Jaubert in his letter to General Bruix (p. 19) says, "Les Arabes et les Mamelouks ont traité quelques-uns des nos prisonniers comme Socrate traitait, dit-on, Alcibiade. Il fallait périr ou y passer."

Old Anglo-Egyptians still chuckle over the tale of Sa'id Pasha and M. de Ruyssenaer, the high-dried and highly respectable Consul-General for the Netherlands, who was solemnly advised to make the experiment, active and passive, before offering his opinion upon the subject. In the present age extensive intercourse with Europeans has produced not a reformation but a certain reticence amongst the upper classes: they are as vicious as ever, but they do not care for displaying their vices to the eyes of mocking strangers.

Syria and Palestine, another ancient focus of abominations, borrowed from Egypt and exaggerated the worship of Androgynic and hermaphroditic deities. Plutarch (De Iside) notes that the old Nilotes held the moon to be of "male-female sex," the men sacrificing to Luna and the women to Lunus.[1] Isis also was a hermaphrodite, the idea being that Aether or Air (the lower heavens) was the menstruum of generative nature; and Damascius explained the tenet by the all-fruitful and prolific powers of the atmosphere. Hence the fragment attributed to Orpheus, the song of Jupiter (Air)—

> All things from Jove descend
> Jove was a male, Jove was a deathless bride;
> For men call Air, of two-fold sex, the Jove.

Julius Firmicus relates that "The Assyrians and part of the Africans" (along the Mediterranean seaboard?) "hold Air to be the chief element and adore its fanciful figure (*imaginata figura*), con-

---

[1] Arnobius and Tertullian, with the arrogance of their caste and its miserable ignorance of that symbolism which often concealed from vulgar eyes the most precious mysteries, used to taunt the heathen for praying to deities whose sex they ignored: "Consuistis in precibus 'Seu tu Deus seu tu Dea,' dicere!" These men would know everything; they made God the merest work of man's brains and armed him with a despotism of omnipotence which rendered their creation truly dreadful.

secrated under the name of Juno or the Virgin Venus. . . . Their companies of priests cannot duly serve her unless they effeminate their faces, smooth their skins and disgrace their masculine sex by feminine ornaments. You may see men in their very temples amid general groans enduring miserable dalliance and becoming passives like women (*viros muliebria pati*) and they expose, with boasting and ostentation, the pollution of the impure and immodest body."

Here we find the religious significance of eunuchry. It was practised as a religious rite by the Tympanotribas or Gallus,[1] the castrated votary of Rhea or Bona Mater, in Phrygia called Cybele, self-mutilated but *not* in memory of Atys; and by a host of other creeds: even Christianity, as sundry texts show,[2] could not alto-

---

[1] Gallus, literally=a cock, in pornologic parlance is a capon, a castrato.

[2] The texts justifying or conjoining castration are Matt. xviii. 8-9; Mark ix. 43-47; Luke xxiii. 29 and Col. iii. 5. St. Paul preached (1 Corin. vii. 29) that a man should live with his wife as if he had none. The Abelian heretics of Africa abstained from women because Abel died virginal. Origen mutilated himself after interpreting too rigorously Matth. xix. 12, and was duly excommunicated. But his disciple, the Arab Valerius founded

gether cast out the old possession. Here too we have an explanation of Sotadic love in its second stage, when it became, like cannibalism, a matter of superstition. Assuming a nature-implanted tendency, we see, that like human sacrifice, it was held to be the most acceptable offering to the God-goddess in the Orgia or sacred ceremonies, a something set apart for peculiar worship. Hence in Rome as in Egypt the temples of Isis (*Inachidos limina, Isiacæ sacraria Lunæ*) were centres of sodomy and the religious practice was adopted by the grand priestly castes from Mesopotamia to Mexico and Peru.

We find the earliest written notices of the Vice in the mythical destruction of the Pentapolis

---

(A.D. 250) the castrated sect called Valerians who, persecuted and dispersed by the Emperors Constantine and Justinian, became the spiritual fathers of the modern Skopzis. These eunuchs first appeared in Russia at the end of the eleventh century, when two Greeks, John and Jephrem, were metropolitans of Kiev; the former was brought thither in A.D. 1089 by Princess Anna Wassewolodowna and is called by the chronicles Nawjè or the Corpse. But early in the eighteenth century (1715-1733) a sect arose in the circle of Uglitseh and in Moscow, at first called Clisti or flagellants, which developed into the modern Skopzi. For this extensive subject see De Stein (Zeitschrift für Ethn. Berlin, 1875) and Mantegazza, chapt. vi.

(Gen. xix.), Sodom, Gomorrah (= 'Amirah, the cultivated country), Adama, Zeboïm and Zoar or Bela. The legend has been amply embroidered by the Rabbis who make the Sodomites do everything *à l'envers: e.g.* if a man were wounded he was fined for bloodshed and compelled to fee the offender; and if one cut off the ear of a neighbor's ass he was condemned to keep the animal till the ear grew again. The Jewish doctors declare the people to have been a race of sharpers with rogues for magistrates, and thus they justify the judgment which they read literally. But the traveller cannot accept it.

I have carefully examined the lands at the North and at the South of that most beautiful lake, the so-called Dead Sea, whose tranquil loveliness, backed by the grand plateau of Moab, is an object of admiration to all save patients suffering from the strange disease "Holy Land on the Brain."[1] But I found no traces of craters in the neighborhood, no signs of vulcanism, no remains of "meteoric stones": the asphalt which named the water is a mineralized vegetable washed out

---

[1] See the marvellously absurd description of the glorious "Dead Sea" in the Purchas v. 84.

of the limestones and the sulphur and salt are brought down by the Jordan into a lake without issue.

I must therefore look upon the history as a myth which may have served a double purpose. The first would be to deter the Jew from the Malthusian practices of his pagan predecessors, upon whom obloquy was thus cast, so far resembling the scandalous and absurd legend which explained the names of the children of Lot by Pheiné and Thamma as "Moab" (Mu-ab) the water or semen of the father, and "Ammon" as mother's son, that is, bastard. The fable would also account for the abnormal fissure containing the lower Jordan and the Dead Sea, which the late Sir R. I. Murchison used wrong-headedly to call a "Volcano of Depression": this geological feature, that cuts off the river-basin from its natural outlet the Gulf of Eloth (Akabah), must date from myriads of years before there were "Cities of the Plain."

But the main object of the ancient lawgiver, Osarsiph, Moses or the Moseidæ, was doubtless to discountenance a perversion prejudicial to the increase of population. And he speaks with no uncertain voice: "Whoso lieth with a beast shall surely be put to death" (Exod. xxii. 19): "If a man lie with mankind as he lieth with a woman, both of them have committed an abomination: they shall surely be put to death; their blood shall be upon them" (Levit. xx. 13; where v.v. 15-16 threaten with death man and woman who lie with beasts). Again: "There shall be no whore of the daughters of Israel nor a sodomite of the sons of Israel" (Deut. xxii. 5).

The old commentators on the Sodom-myth are most unsatisfactory, *e.g.* Parkhurst, *s.v.* Kadesh. "From hence we may observe the peculiar propriety of this punishment of Sodom and of the neighboring cities. By their sodomitical impurities they meant to acknowledge the Heavens as the cause of fruitfulness independently upon, and in opposition to Jehovah[1]; therefore Jehovah, by raining upon them not genial showers but brim-

---

[1] Jehovah here is made to play an evil part by destroying men instead of teaching them better. But, "Nous faisons les Dieux, à notre image et nous portons dans le ciel ce que nous voyons sur la terre." The idea of Yahweh, or Yah is palpably Egyptian, the Ankh or ever-living One: the etymon, however, was learned at Babylon and is still found amongst the cuneiforms.

THE SOTADIC ZONE ᵌ ᵌ ᵌ 57

stone from heaven, not only destroyed the inhabitants, but also changed all that country, which was before as the garden of God, into brimstone and salt that is not sown nor beareth, neither any grass groweth therein." It must be owned that to this Pentapolis was dealt very hard measure for religiously and diligently practising a popular rite which a host of cities, even in the present day, as Naples and Shiraz, to mention no others, affect for simple luxury and affect with impunity. The myth may probably reduce itself to very small proportions, a few Fellah villages destroyed by a storm, like that which drove Brennus from Delphi.

The Hebrews entering Syria found it religionized by Assyria and Babylonia, whence Accadian Ishtar had passed west and had become Ashtoreth, Ashtaroth or Ashirah,[1] the Anaitis of Armenia, the Phœnician Astarte and the Greek Aphrodite, the great Moon-goddess[2] who is queen

---

[1] The name still survives in the Shajarát al-Ashará, a clump of trees near the village Al-Ghájar (of the Gypsies?) at the foot of Hermon.

[2] I am not quite sure that Astarte is not primarily the planet Venus; but I can hardly doubt that Professor Max Müller and

of Heaven and Love. In another phase she was Venus Mylitta = the Procreatrix, in Chaldaic Mauludatà and in Arabic Moawallidah, she who bringeth forth. She was worshipped by men habited as women and vice versâ; for which reason in the Torah (Deut. xx. 5) the sexes are forbidden to change dress. The male prostitutes were called Kadesh the holy, the woman being Kadeshah, and doubtless gave themselves up to great excesses.

Eusebius (De bit. Const. iii. c. 55) describes a school of impurity at Aphac, where women and "men who were not men" practised all manner of abominations in honor of the Demon (Venus). Here the Phrygian symbolism of Kybele and Attis (Atys) had become the Syrian Ba'al Tammuz and Astarte, and the Grecian Dionæa and Adonis, the anthropomorphic forms of the two greater lights. The site, Apheca, now Wady al-Afik on the route from Bayrut to the Cedars, is

---

Sir G. Cox are mistaken in bringing from India Aphrodite the Dawn and her attendants, the Charities identified with the Vedic Harits. Of Ishtar in Accadia, however, Roscher seems to have proved that she is distinctly the Moon sinking into Amenti (the west, the Underworld) in search of her lost spouse Izdubar, the Sun-god. This again is pure Egyptianism.

THE SOTADIC ZONE 59

a glen of wild and wondrous beauty, fitting frame-work for the loves of goddess and demigod: and the ruins of the temple destroyed by Constantine contrast with Nature's work, the glorious fountain, *splendidior vitro,* which feeds the River Ibrahim and still at times Adonis runs purple to the sea.[1]

The Phœnicians spread this androgynic worship over Greece. We find the consecrated servants and votaries of Corinthian Aphrodite called Hierodouli (Strabo viii. 6), who aided the ten thousand courtesans in gracing the Venus-

---

[1] In this classical land of Venus the worship of Ishtar-Ashtaroth is by no means obsolete. The Metáwali heretics, a people of Persian descent and Shiite tenets, and the peasantry of "Bilád B'sharrah," which I would derive from Bayt Ashirah, still pilgrimage to the ruins and address their vows to the Sayyidat al-Kabirah, the Great Lady. Orthodox Moslems accuse them of abominable orgies and point to the lamps and rags which they suspend to a tree entitled Shajarat al-Sitt—the Lady's tree—an Acacia Albida which, according to some travellers, is found only here and at Sayda (Sidon) where an avenue exists. The people of Kasrawán, a Christian province in the Libanus, inhabited by a peculiarly prurient race, also hold high festival under the far-famed Cedars and their women sacrifice to Venus like the Kadashah of the Phœnicians. This survival of old superstition is unknown to missionary "Handbooks," but amply deserves the study of the anthropologist.

temple: from this excessive luxury arose the proverb popularized by Horace. One of the headquarters of the cult was Cyprus where, as Servius relates (Ad Æn. ii. 632), stood the simulacre of a bearded Aphrodite with feminine body and costume, sceptered and mitred like a man. The sexes when worshiping it exchanged habits and here the virginity was offered in sacrifice: Herodotus (i. c. 199) describes this defloration at Babylon but sees only the shameful part of the custom which was a mere consecration of a tribal rite. Everywhere girls before marriage belong either to the father or to the clan and thus the maiden paid the debt due to the public before becoming private property as a wife. The same usage prevailed in ancient Armenia and in parts of Ethiopia; and Herodotus tells us that a practice very much like the Babylonian "is found also in certain parts of the Island of Cyprus:" it is noticed by Justin (xviii. c. 5) and probably explains the "Succoth Benoth" or Damsels' booths which the Babylonians transplanted to the cities of Samaria.[1]

---

[1] Some commentators understand "the tabernacles sacred to the reproductive powers of women"; and the Rabbis declare that the emblem was the figure of a setting hen.

THE SOTADIC ZONE 61

The Jews seem very successfully to have copied the abominations of their pagan neighbors, even in the matter of the "dog."[1] In the reign of wicked Rehoboam (B.C. 975) "There were also sodomites in the land and they did according to all the abominations of the nations which the Lord cast out before the children of Israel" (1 Kings xiv. 20). The scandal was abated by zealous King Asa (B.C. 958) whose grandmother[2] was high-priestess of Priapus (*princeps in sacris Priapi*): he "took away the sodomites out of the land (1 Kings xv. 12). Yet the prophets were loud in their complaints, especially the so-called Isaiah (B.C. 760), "except the Lord of Hosts had left to us a very small remnant, we should have

---

[1] "Dog" is applied by the older Jews to the Sodomite and the Catamite; and thus they understand the "price of a dog" which could not be brought into the Temple (Deut. xxiii. 18). I have noticed it in one of the derivations of *cinædus* and can only remark that it is a vile libel upon the canine tribe.

[2] Her name was Maachah and her title, according to some, "King's mother": she founded the sect of Communists who rejected marriage and made adultery and incest part of worship in their splendid temple. Such were the Basilians and the Carpocratians, followed in the eleventh century by Tranchelin, whose sectarians, the Turlupins, long infested Savoy.

been as Sodom" (i. 9); and strong measures were required from good King Josiah (B.C. 641) who amongst other things, "brake down the houses of the sodomites that were by the house of the Lord, where the women wove hangings for the grove" (2 Kings xxiii. 7). The *bordels* of boys (*peuris alienis adhæseverunt*) had been near the Temple.

Syria has not forgotten her old "praxis." At Damascus I found some noteworthy cases among the religious of the great Amawi Mosque. As for the Druses we have Burckhardt's authority (Travels in Syria, etc., p. 202) "unnatural propensities are very common amongst them."

The Sotadic Zone covers the whole of Asia Minor and Mesopotamia now occupied by the "unspeakable Turk," a race of born pederasts; and in the former region we first notice a peculiarity of the feminine figure, the *mammæ inclinatæ, jacentes et pannosæ,* which prevails over all this part of the belt. Whilst the women to the North and South have, with local exceptions, the *mammæ stantes* of the European virgin,[1] those of

---

[1] A noted exception is Vienna, remarkable for the enormous development of the virginal bosom, which soon becomes pendulent.

Turkey, Persia, Afghanistan and Kashmir lose all the fine curves of the bosom, sometimes even before the first child; and after it the hemispheres take the form of bags. This cannot result from climate only; the women of Marathâ-land, inhabiting a damper and hotter region than Kashmir, are noted for fine firm breasts even after parturition.

The Vice, of course, prevails more in the cities and towns of Asiatic Turkey than in the villages; yet even these are infected; while the nomad Turcomans contrast badly in this point with the Gypsies, those Badawin of India. The Kurd population is of Iranian origin, which means that the evil is deeply rooted: I have noted in the Arabian Nights that the great and glorious Saladin was a habitual pederast. The Armenians, as their national character is, will prostitute themselves for gain but prefer women to boys: Georgia supplied Turkey with catamites while Circassia sent concubines. In Mesopotamia the barbarous invader has almost obliterated the ancient civilization which is antedated only by the Nilotic: the mysteries of old Babylon nowhere survive save in certain obscure tribes like the

Mandæans, the Devil-worshippers and the Ali-iláhi.

Entering Persia we find the reverse of Armenia; and, despite Herodotus, I believe that Iran borrowed her pathologic love from the peoples of the Tigris Euphrates Valley and not from the then insignificant Greeks. But whatever may be its origin, the corruption is now bred in the bone. It begins in boyhood and many Persians account for it by paternal severity. Youths arrived at puberty find none of the facilities with which Europe supplies fornication. Onanism[1] is to a certain extent discouraged by circumcision, and meddling with the father's slave-girls and concubines would be risking cruel punishment if not death. Hence they use each other by turns, a "puerile practice" known as Alish-Takish, the Latin *facere vicibus* or *Mutuum facere*. Temperament, media, and atavism recommend the custom to the general; and after marrying and begetting heirs, Paterfamilias returns to the Gany-

---

[1] Gen. xxxviii. 2-11. Amongst the classics Mercury taught the "Art of le Thalaba" to his son Pan, who wandered about the mountains distraught with love for the Nymph Echo and Pan passed it on to the pastors. See Thalaba in Mirabeau.

THE SOTADIC ZONE ⌒ ⌒ ⌒ 65

mede. Hence all the odes of Hafiz are addressed to youths, as proved by such Arabic exclamations as 'Afáka 'llah=Allah assain thee (masculine)[1]: the object is often fanciful but it would be held coarse and immodest to address an imaginary girl.[2]

An illustration of the penchant is told at Shiraz concerning a certain Mujtahid, the head of the Shi'ah creed, corresponding with a prince-archbishop in Europe. A friend once said to him, "There is a question I would fain address to your Eminence but I lack the daring to do so." "Ask and fear not," replied the Divine. "It is this, O Mujtahid! Figure thee in a garden of roses and hyacinths with the evening breeze waving the cypress-heads, a fair youth of twenty sitting by thy side and the assurance of perfect privacy. What, prithee, would be the result?" The holy man bowed the chin of doubt upon the collar of

---

[1] The reader of the Arabian Nights has remarked how often the "he" in Arabic poetry denotes a "she"; but the Arab, when uncontaminated by travel, ignores pederasty, and the Arab poet is a Badawi.

[2] So Mohammed addressed his girl-wife Ayishah in the masculine.

meditation; and, too honest to lie, presently whispered, "Allah defend me from such temptation of Satan!"

Yet even in Persia men have not been wanting who have done their utmost to uproot the Vice: in the same Shiraz they speak of a father who, finding his son in flagrant delict, put him to death like Brutus or Lynch of Galway. Such isolated cases, however, can effect nothing. Chardin tells us that houses of male prostitution were common in Persia whilst those of women were unknown: the same is the case in the present day and the boys are prepared with extreme care by diet, baths, depilation, unguents and a host of artists in cosmetics.[1]

The Vice is looked upon at most as a peccadillo and its mention crops up in every jest-book. When the Isfahan man mocked Shaykh Sa'adi, by comparing the bald pates of Shirazian elders

---

[1] So amongst the Romans we have the Iatroliptæ, youths or girls who wiped the gymnast's perspiring body with swan-down, a practice renewed by the professors of "Massage"; Unctores, who applied perfumes and essences; Fricatrices and Tractatrices or shampooers; Dropacistæ, corn-cutters; Alipilarii, who plucked the hair, etc., etc., etc.

to the bottom of a lotá, a brass cup with a wide-necked opening used in the Hammam, the witty poet turned its aperture upwards and thereto likened the well-abused podex of an Isfahani youth. Another favorite piece of Shirazian "chaff" is to declare that when an Isfahan father would set up his son in business he provides him with a pound of rice, meaning that he can sell the result as compost for the kitchen-garden, and with the price buy another meal: hence the saying Khakh-i-pái káhú = the soil at the lettuce-root. The Isfahanis retort with the name of a station or halting-place between the two cities where, under pretence of making travellers stow away their riding-gear, many a Shirázi had been raped: hence "Zín o takaltú tú bi-bar" = carry within saddle and saddle-cloth!

A favorite Persian punishment for strangers caught in the Harem or Gynæceum is to strip and throw them and expose them to the embraces of the grooms and negro-slaves. I once asked a Shirazi how penetration was possible if the patient resisted with all the force of the sphincter muscle: he smiled and said, "Ah, we Persians know a trick to get over that; we apply a sharpened tent-peg to the crupper-bone (*os coccygis*) and knock till he opens." A well-known missionary to the East during the last generation was subjected to this gross insult by one of the Persian Prince-governors, whom he had infuriated by his conversion-mania: in his memoirs he alludes to it by mentioning his "dishonored person"; but English readers cannot comprehend the full significance of the confession.

About the same time Shaykh Nasr, Governor of Bushire, a man famed for facetious blackguardism, used to invite European youngsters serving in the Bombay Marine and ply them with liquor till they were insensible. Next morning the middies mostly complained that the champagne had caused a curious irritation and soreness in *la parte-poste*.

The same Eastern "Scrogin" would ask his guests if they had ever seen a man-cannon (Adami-top); and, on their replying in the negative, a grey-beard slave was dragged in blaspheming and struggling with all his strength. He was presently placed on all fours and firmly held by the extremities; his bag-trousers were let down and a dozen peppercorns were inserted *ano suo*:

THE SOTADIC ZONE 69

the target was a sheet of paper held at a reasonable distance; the match was applied by a pinch of cayenne in the nostrils, the sneeze started the grapeshot and the number of hits on the butt decided the bets.

We can hardly wonder at the loose conduct of Persian women perpetually mortified by marital pederasty. During the unhappy campaign of 1856-57 in which, with the exception of a few brilliant skirmishes, we gained no glory, Sir James Outram and the Bombay army showing how bad they were, there was a formal outburst of the Harems; and even women of princely birth could not be kept out of the officers' quarters.

The cities of Afghanistan and Sind are thoroughly saturated with Persian vice, and the people sing

>   Kadr-i-kus Aughán dánad, kadr-i-kunrá Kábuli:
>   The worth of c—— the Afghan knows: Cabul
>   prefers the other *chose!*[1]

---

[1] It is a parody on the well-known song (Roebuck 1, sect 2, No. 1602):

>   The goldsmith knows the worth of gold, jewellers
>   worth of jewelry;
>   The worth of rose Bulbul can tell and Kambar's
>   worth his lord, Ali.

The Afghans are commercial travellers on a large scale and each caravan is accompanied by a number of boys and lads almost in woman's attire with *kohl'd* eyes and rouged cheeks, long tresses and henna'd fingers and toes, riding luxuriously in Kajáwas or camel-panniers: they are called Kúch-i safari, or travelling wives, and the husbands trudge patiently by their sides. In Afghanistan also a frantic debauchery broke out amongst the women when they found *incubi* who were not pederasts; and the scandal was not the most insignificant cause of the general rising at Cabul (Nov. 1841).

Resuming our way Eastward we find the Sikhs and the Moslems of the Panjab much addicted to the Vice, although the Himalayan tribes to the north and those lying south, the Rájputs and Marathás, ignore it. The same may be said of the Kashmirians who add another Kappa to the tria Kakista, Kappadocians, Kretans, and Kilicians: the proverb says,

Agar kaht-i-mardum uftad, az ín sih jins kam gírí;
Eki Afghán, dovvum Sindí,[1] siyyum badjins-i-Kashmírí:

Though of men there be famine yet shun these three—
Afghan, Sindi and rascally Kashmírí.

Louis Daville describes the infamies of Lahore and Lakhnau where he found men dressed as women, with flowing locks under crowns of flowers, imitating the feminine walk and gestures, voice and fashion of speech, and ogling their admirers with all the coquetry of *bayadères*. Victor Jacquemont's Journal de Voyage describes the pederasty of Ranjít Singh, the "Lion of the Panjáb," and his pathic Guláb Singh whom the English inflicted upon Cashmir as ruler by way of paying for his treason. Yet the Hindus, I repeat, hold pederasty in abhorrence and are as much scandalized by being called Gánd-márá (anus-beater) or Gándú (anuser) as Englishmen would be.

During the years 1843-44 my regiment, almost all Hindu Sepoys of the Bombay Presidency, was stationed at a purgatory called Bandar Ghárrá,[2] a sandy flat with a scatter of verdigris-green milk-bush some forty miles north of Karáchi the headquarters. The dirty heap of mud-and-mat hovels,

---

[1] For "Sindí" Roebuck (Oriental Proverbs Part i. p. 99) has Kunbu (Kumboh) a Panjábi peasant and others vary the saying *ad libitum*.

[2] See 'Sind Revisited" i. 133-35.

which represented the adjacent native village, could not supply a single woman; yet only one case of pederasty came to light and that after a tragical fashion some years afterwards. A young Brahman had connection with a soldier comrade of low caste and this had continued till, in an unhappy hour, the Pariah patient ventured to become the agent. The latter, in Arab. Al-Fá'il = the "doer," is not an object of contempt like Al-Mafúl = the "done"; and the high-caste sepoy, stung by remorse and revenge, loaded his musket and deliberately shot his paramour. He was hanged by court martial at Hyderabad and, when his last wishes were asked, he begged in vain to be suspended by the feet; the idea being that his soul, polluted by exciting "below the waist," would be doomed to endless transmigrations through the lowest forms of life.

Beyond India, I have stated, the Sotadic Zone begins to broaden out embracing all China, Turkistan and Japan. The Chinese, as far as we know them in the great cities, are omnivorous and omnifutuentes: they are the chosen people of debauchery and their systematic bestiality with ducks, goats, and other animals is equalled only

THE SOTADIC ZONE 73

by their pederasty. Kæmpfer and Orlof Torée (Voyage en Chine) notice their public houses for boys. Mirabeau (L'Anandryne) describes the tribadism of their women in hammocks.

When Pekin was plundered the Harems contained a number of balls a little larger than the old musket-bullet, made of thin silver with a loose pellet of brass inside somewhat like a grelot[1]: these articles were placed by the women between the labia and an up-and-down movement on the bed gave a pleasant titillation when nothing better was to be procured.

They have every artifice of luxury, aphrodisiacs, erotic perfumes and singular applications. Such are the pills which, dissolved in water and applied to the *glans penis,* cause it to throb and swell: so according to Amerigo Vespucci, American women could artificially increase the size of their husbands' parts.[2] The Chinese bracelet of

---

[1] They must not be confounded with the *grelots lascifs,* the little bells of gold or silver set by the people of Pegu in the prepuce-skin, and described by Nicolo de Conti who, however, refused to undergo the operation.

[2] Relation des découvertes faites par Colomb, etc. p. 137: Bologna 1875: also Vespucci's letter in Ramusio (i. 131) and Paro's Recherches philosophiques sur les Américains.

caoutchouc studded with points now takes the place of the Herisson, or *Annulus hirsutus*,[1] which was bound between the *glans* and prepuce. Of the *penis succedaneus*, that imitation of the Arbor vitæ or Soter Kosmou, which the Latins called *phallus* and *fascinum*,[2] the French *godemiché* and the Italians *passatempo* and *diletto* (whence our "dildo"), every kind abounds, varying from a stuffed "French letter" to a cone of ribbed horn which looks like an instrument of torture. For the use of men they have the "merkin,"[3] a heart-shaped article of thin skin stuffed with cotton and slit with an artificial vagina: two tapes at the top and one below, lash it to the back of a chair.

[1] See Mantegazza, referred to before, who borrows from the Thèse de Paris of Dr. Abel Hureau de Villeneuve, "Frictiones per coitum productæ magnum mucosæ membranæ vaginalis turgorem, ac simul hujus cuniculi coarctationem tam maritis salacibus quæritatam afferunt."

[2] Fascinus is the Priapus-god to whom the Vestal Virgins of Rome, professed tribades, sacrificed; also the neck-charm in phallus-shape. Fascinum is the male member.

[3] Captain Grose (Lexicon Balatronicum) explains merkin as "counterfeit hair for women's privy parts. See Bailey's Dict." The Bailey of 1764, an "improved edition," does not contain the word which is now generally applied to a *cunnus succedaneus*.

THE SOTADIC ZONE ～ ～ ～ 75

The erotic literature of the Chinese and Japanese is highly developed and their illustrations are often facetious as well as obscene. All are familiar with that of the strong man who by a blow with his enormous phallus shivers a copper pot; and the ludicrous contrast of the huge-membered wights who land in the Isle of Women and presently escape from it, wrinkled and shrivelled, true Domine Dolittles.

Of Turkistan we know little, but what we know confirms my statement. Mr. Schuyler in his Turkistan (i. 132) offers an illustration of a "Batchah" (Pers. bachcheh = catamite), "or singing-boy surrounded by his admirers." Of the Tartars Master Purchas laconically says (v. 419), "They are addicted to Sodomie or Buggerie."

The learned casuist Dr. Thomas Sanchez, the Spaniard, had (says Mirabeau in Kadhésch) to decide a difficult question concerning the sinfulness of a peculiar erotic perversion. The Jesuits brought home from Manilla a tailed man whose moveable prolongation of the *os coccygis* measured from 7 to 10 inches: he had placed himself between two women, enjoying one naturally while the other used his tail as a *penis succe-daneus*. The verdict was incomplete sodomy and simple fornication.

For the islands north of Japan, the "Sodomitical Sea," and the "nayle of tynne" thrust through the prepuce to prevent sodomy, see Lib. ii. chap. 4 of Master Thomas Caudish's Circumnavigation, and vol. vi. of Pinkerton's Geography translated by Walckenaer.

Passing over to America we find that the Sotadic Zone contains the whole hemisphere from Behring Straits to Magellan's. This prevalence of "mollities" astonishes the anthropologist, who is apt to consider pederasty the growth of luxury and the especial product of great and civilized cities, unnecessary and therefore unknown to simple savagery where the births of both sexes are about equal and female infanticide is not practised. In many parts of the New World this perversion was accompanied by another depravity of taste—confirmed cannibalism.[1] The forests and *campos* abounded in game from

---

[1] I have noticed this phenomenal cannibalism in my notes to Albert Tootle's excellent translation of "The Captivity of Hans Stade of Hesse": London, Hakluyt Society, 1874.

the deer to the pheasant-like penelope, and the seas and rivers produced an unfailing supply of excellent fish and shell-fish[1]; yet the Brazilian Tupis preferred the meat of man to every other food.

A glance at Bancroft[2] proves the abnormal development of sodomy amongst the savages and barbarians of the New World. Even his half-frozen Hyperboreans "possess all the passions which are supposed to develop most freely under a milder temperature" (i. 58). "The voluptuousness and polygamy of the North American Indians, under a temperature of almost perpetual winter is far greater than that of the most sensual tropical nations" (Martin's Brit. Colonies iii. 524). I can quote only a few of the most remarkable instances.

Of the Koniagas of Kadiak Island and the Thinkleets we read (i. 81-82), "The most repugnant of all their practices is that of male con-

---

[1] The Ostreiras or shell mounds of the Brazil, sometimes 200 feet high, are described by me in Anthropologia No. i. Oct., 1873.

[2] The Native Races of the Pacific States of South America, by Herbert Howe Bancroft, London, Longmans, 1875.

cubinage. A Kadiak mother will select her handsomest and most promising boy, and dress and rear him as a girl, teaching him only domestic duties, keeping him at women's work, associating him with women and girls, in order to render his effeminacy complete. Arriving at the age of ten or fifteen years, he is married to some wealthy man who regards such a companion as a great acquisition. These male concubines are called Achnutschik or Schopans" (the authorities quoted being Holmberg, Langsdorff, Billing, Choris, Lisiansky and Marchand).

The same is the case in Nutka Sound and the Aleutian Islands, where "male concubinage obtains throughout, but not to the same extent as amongst the Koniagas." The objects of "unnatural" affection have their beards carefully plucked out as soon as the face-hair begins to grow, and their chins are tattooed like those of the women.

In California the first missionaries found the same practice, the youths being called Joya (Bancroft, i. 415 and authorities Palon, Crespi, Boscana, Mofras, Torquemada, Duflot and Fages). The Comanches unite incest with sodomy (i. 515). "In New Mexico according to Arlegui,

Ribas, and other authors, male concubinage prevails to a great extent, these loathsome semblances of humanity, whom to call beastly were a slander upon beasts, dress themselves in the clothes and perform the functions of women, the use of weapons being denied them" (i. 585).

Pederasty was systematically practised by the peoples of Cueba, Careta, and other parts of Central America. The Caciques and some of the headmen kept harems of youths who, as soon as destined for the unclean office, were dressed as women. They went by the name of Camayoas, and were hated and detested by the good wives (i. 773-74). Of the Nahua nations Father Pierre de Gand (alias de Musa) writes, "Un certain nombre de prêtres n'avaient point de femmes, *sed eorum loco pueros quibus abutebantur*. Ce péché était si commun dans ce pays que, jeunes ou vieux, tous étaient infectés; ils y étaient si adonnés que mêmes les enfants de six ans s'y livraient" (Ternaux-Campans, Voyages, Série i Tom. x. p. 197).

Among the Mayas of Yucatan Las Casas declares that the great prevalence of "unnatural" lust made parents anxious to see their progeny wedded as soon as possible (Kingsborough's Mex. Ant. viii. 135). In Vera Paz a god, called by some Chin and by others Cavial and Maran, taught it by committing the act with another god. Some fathers gave their sons a boy to use as a woman, and if any other approached this pathic he was treated as an adulterer. In Yucatan images were found by Bernal Diaz proving the sodomitical propensities of the people (Bancroft v. 198). De Pauw (Recherches Philosophiques sur les Américans, London, 1771) has much to say about the subject in Mexico generally: in the northern provinces men married youths who, dressed like women, were forbidden to carry arms. According to Gomara there were at Tamualipas houses of male prostitution; and from Diaz and others we gather that the *pecado nefando* was the rule. Both in Mexico and in Peru it might have caused, if it did not justify, the cruelties of the Conquistadores. Pederasty was also general throughout Nicaragua, and the early explorers found it amongst the indigenes of Panama.

We have authentic details concerning the Vice in Peru and its adjacent lands, beginning with Cieza de Leon, who must be read in the original or in the translated extracts of Purchas (vol. v. 942, etc.), not in the cruelly castrated form preferred by the Council of the Hakluyt Society. Speaking of the New Granada Indians he tells us that "at Old Port (Puerto Viejo) and Puna, the Deuill so farre prevayled in their beastly Deuotions that there were Boyes consecrated to serue in the Temple; and at the times of their Sacrifices and Solemne Feasts, the Lords and principall men abused them to that detestable filthinesse"; *i.e.* performed their peculiar worship.

Generally in the hill-countries the Devil, under the show of holiness, had introduced the practice; for every temple or chief house of adoration kept one or two men or more which were attired like women, even from the time of their childhood, and spake like them, imitating them in everything; with these, under pretext of holiness and religion, their principal men on principal days had commerce. Speaking of the arrival of the Giants[1] at Point Santa Elena, Cieza says (chap.

---

[1] All Peruvian historians mention these giants, who were probably the large-limbed Caribs (Caraíbes) of Brazil.

lii.), they were detested by the natives, because in using their women they killed them, and their men also in another way. All the natives declare that God brought upon them a punishment proportioned to the enormity of their offence. When they were engaged together in their accursed intercourse, a fearful and terrible fire came down from Heaven with a great noise, out of the midst of which there issued a shining Angel with a glittering sword, wherewith at one blow they were all killed and the fire consumed them.[1] There remained a few bones and skulls which God allowed to bide unconsumed by the fire, as a memorial of this punishment.

In the Hakluyt Society's bowdlerization we read of the Tumbez Islanders being "very vicious, many of them committing the abominable offence" (p. 24); also, "If by the advice of the Devil any Indian commit the abominable crime, it is thought little of and they call him a woman." In chapters lii. and lviii. we find exceptions. The Indians of Huancabamba, "although so near the peoples of Puerto Viejo and Guayaquil, do not

---

[1] This sounds much like a pious fraud of the missionaries, a Europeo-American version of the Sodom legend.

commit the abominable sin"; and the Serranos, or island mountaineers, as sorcerers and magicians inferior to the coast peoples, were not so much addicted to sodomy.

The Royal Commentaries of the Yncas shows that the evil was of a comparatively modern growth. In the early period of Peruvian history the people considered the crime "unspeakable": if a Cuzco Indian, not of Yncarial blood, angrily addressed the term pederast to another, he was held infamous for many days. One of the generals having reported to the Ynca Ccapacc Yupanqui that there were some sodomites, not in all the valleys, but one here and one there, "nor was it a habit of all the inhabitants but only of certain persons who practised it privately," the ruler ordered that the criminals should be publicly burnt alive and their houses, crops and trees destroyed: moreover, to show his abomination, he commanded that the whole village should so be treated if one man fell into this habit (Lib. iii. cap. 13). Elsewhere we learn, "There were sodomites in some provinces, though not openly nor universally, but some particular men and in secret. In some parts they had them in their temples, because the Devil persuaded them that the Gods took great delight in such people, and thus the Devil acted as a traitor to remove the veil of shame that the Gentiles felt for this crime and to accustom them to commit it in public and in common."

During the times of the Conquistadores male concubinage had become the rule throughout Peru. At Cuzco, we are told by Nuno de Guzman in 1530, "The last which was taken, and which fought most couragiously, was a man in the habite of a woman, which confessed that from a childe he had gotten his liuing by that filthinesse, for which I caused him to be burned." V. F. Lopez[1] draws a frightful picture of pathologic love in Peru. Under the reigns which followed that of Inti-Kapak (Ccapacc) Amauri, the country was attacked by invaders of a giant race coming from the sea: they practised pederasty after a fashion so shameless that the conquered tribes were compelled to fly (p. 271). Under the pre-Yncarial Amauta, or priestly dynasty, Peru had lapsed into savagery and the kings of

---

[1] Les Races Aryennes du Pérou, Paris, Franck, 1871.

THE SOTADIC ZONE 85

Cuzco preserved only the name.[1] When Sinchi Roko (the xcvth of Montesinos and the xcist of Garcilazo) became Ynca, he found morals at the lowest ebb.[2]

I have remarked that the various Tupi races of Brazil were infamous for cannibalism and sodomy; nor could the latter be only racial as proved

---

[1] "Toutes ces hontes et toutes ces misères provenaient de deux vices infâmes, la bestialité et la sodomie. Les femmes surtout étaient offensées de voir la nature frustrée de tous ses droits. Elles pleuraient ensemble en leurs réunions sur le misérable état dans lequel elles étaient tombées, sur le mépris avec lequel elles étaient traitées. . . . Le monde était renversé, les hommes s'aimaient et étaient jaloux les uns des autres. . . . Elles cherchaient, mais en vain, les moyens de remédier au mal; elles employaient des herbes et des recettes diaboliques qui leur ramenaient bien quelques individus, mais ne pouvaient arrêter les progrès incessants du vice. Cet état de choses constitua un véritable moyen âge, qui dura jusqu'à l'établissement du gouvernement des Incas" (p. 277).

[2] "Ni la prudence de l'Inca, ni les lois sévères qu'il avait promulguées n'avaient pu extirper entièrement le péché contre nature. Il reprit avec une nouvelle violence, et les femmes en furent si jalouses qu'un grand nombre d'elles tuèrent leurs maris. Les devins et les sorciers passaient leurs journées à fabriquer, avec certaines herbes, des compositions magiques qui rendaient fous ceux qui en mangaient, et les femmes en faisaient prendre, soit dans les aliments, soit dans la chicha, à ceux dont elles étaient jalouses" (p. 291).

by the fact that colonists of pure Lusitanian blood followed in the path of the savages. Antonio Augusto da Costa Aguiar[1] is outspoken upon this point. "A crime which in England leads to the gallows, and which is the very measure of abject depravity, passes with impunity amongst us by the participating in it of almost all or of many (*de quasi todos, ou de muitos.*) Ah! if the wrath of Heaven were to fall by way of punishing such crimes (*delictos*), more than one city of this Empire, more than a dozen, would pass into the category of the Sodoms and Gomorrahs" (p. 30). Till late years pederasty in Brazil was looked upon as a peccadillo; the European immigrants following the practice of the wild men who were naked but not, as Columbus said, clothed in innocence. One of Her Majesty's Consuls used to tell a tale of the hilarity provoked in a "fashionable" assembly by the open declaration of a young gentleman that his mulatto "patient" had suddenly turned upon him, insisting upon becoming agent. Now, however, under the influences of improved education and respect for the

---

[1] O Brazil e os Brazileiros, Santos, 1862.

THE SOTADIC ZONE 87

public opinion of Europe, pathologic love amongst the Luso-Brazilians, has been reduced to the normal limits.

Outside the Sotadic Zone, I have said, the Vice is sporadic, not endemic: yet the physical and moral effect of great cities where puberty, they say, is induced earlier than in country sites, has been the same in most lands, causing modesty to decay and pederasty to flourish. The Badawi Arab is wholly pure of the Vice, yet San'á the capital of Al-Yaman and other centres of population have long been and still are thoroughly infected. History tells us of Zú Shanátir, tyrant of "Arabia Felix," in A.D. 478, who used to entice young men into his palace and cause them after use to be cast out of the windows: this unkindly ruler was at last poniarded by the youth Zerash, known from his long ringlets as "Zú Nowás." The negro race is mostly untainted by sodomy and tribadism. Yet Joan dos Sanctos[1] found in Cacongo of West Africa "Chibudi, which are men attyred like women and behaue themselves womanly, ashamed to be called men; are also mar-

---

[1] Aethiopia Orientalis, Purchas ii. 1558.

ried to men, and esteem that vnnaturale damnation an honor." Madagascar also delighted in dancing and singing boys dressed as girls. In the Empire of Dahomey I noted a corps of prostitutes kept for the use of the Amazon-soldieresses.

North of the Sotadic Zone we find local but notable instances. Master Christopher Burrough[1] describes on the western side of the Volga "a very fine stone castle, called by the name Oueak, and adioyning to the same a Towne called by the *Russes, Sodom,* ... which was swallowed into the earth for the wickednesse of the people."

Again: although as a rule Christianity has steadily opposed pathologic love both in writing and preaching, there have been remarkable exceptions. Perhaps the most curious idea was that of certain medical writers in the middle ages: "Usus et amplexus pueri, bene temperatus, salutaris medicina" (Tardieu). Bayle notices (under "Vayer" the infamous Book of Giovanni della Casa, Archbishop of Benevento, "De laudibus Sodomiæ,"[2] vulgarly

---

[1] Purchas iii. 243.

[2] For a literal translation see Premiere Série de la Curiosité Littéraire et Bibliographique, Paris, Liseux, 1880.

known as "Capitolo del Forno." The same writer refers (under "Sixte iv") to the report that the Dominican Order, which systematically decried the Vice, had presented a request to the Cardinal di Santa Lucia that sodomy might be lawful during three months per annum, June to August; and that the Cardinal had underwritten the petition "Be it done as they demand." Hence the Fæda Venus of Battista Mantovano. Bayle rejects the history for a curious reason, venery being colder in summer than in winter, and quotes the proverb "Aux mois qui n'ont pas d' R, peu embrasser et bien boire." But in the case of a celibate priesthood such scandals are inevitable: witness the famous Jesuit epitaph: *Ci-gît un Jésuite,* etc.

In our modern capitals, London, Berlin and Paris, for instance, the Vice seems subject to periodical outbreaks. For many years, also, England sent her pederasts to Italy, and especially to Naples whence originated the term "Il vizio Inglese." It would be invidious to detail the scandals which of late years have startled the public in London and Dublin: for these the curious will consult the police reports.

Berlin, despite her strong flavor of Pharisee-ism, Puritanism and Chauvinism in religion, manners and morals, is not a whit better than her neighbors. Dr. Gaspar,[1] a well-known authority on the subject, adduces many interesting cases especially an old Count Cajus and his six accomplices. Amongst his many correspondents one suggested to him that not only Plato and Julius Cæsar but also Winckelmann and Platen (?) belonged to the Society; and he had found it flourishing in Palermo, the Louvre, the Scottish Highlands and St. Petersburg, to name only a few places.

Frederick the Great is said to have addressed these words to his nephew, "Je puis vous assurer, par mon expérience personelle, que ce plaisir est peu agréable à cultiver." This suggests the popular anecdote of Voltaire and the Englishman who agreed upon an "experience" and found it far from satisfactory. A few days afterwards the latter informed the Sage of Ferney that he had attempted it again and provoked the caustic

---

[1] His best known works are (1) Praktisches Handbuch der Gerechtlichen Medecin, Berlin, 1860; and (2) Klinische Novellen zur gerechtlichen Medecin, Berlin, 1863.

reply: "Once a philosopher; twice a sodomite!"

The last revival of the kind in Germany is a society at Frankfort and its neighborhood self-styled Les Cravates Noires in opposition, I suppose, to Les Cravates Blanches of A. Belot.

Paris is by no means more depraved than Berlin and London; but, whilst the latter hushes up the scandal, Frenchmen do not: hence we see a more copious account of it submitted to the public. For France of the seventeenth century consult the "Histoire de la Prostitution chez tous les Peuples du Monde," and "La France devenue Italienne," a treatise which generally follows "L'Histoire Amoureuse des Gaules" by Bussy, Comte de Rabutin.[1] The headquarters of male prostitution were then in the Champ Flory, *i.e.*, Champ de Flore, the privileged rendezvous of low courtesans. In the eighteenth century, "quand le Française à tête folle," as Voltaire sings, invented the term "Péché philosophique,"

---

[1] The same author printed another imitation of Petronius Arbiter, the "Larissa" story of Théophile Viand. His cousin, the Sévigné, highly approved of it. See Bayle's objections to Rabutin's delicacy and excuses for Petronius' grossness in his "Eclaircissement sur les obscénités" (Appendice au Dictionnaire Antique).

there was a temporary recrudescence; and, after the death of Pidauzet de Mairobert (March, 1779), his "Apologie de la Secte Anandryne" was published in L'Espion Anglais. In those days the Allée des Veuves in the Champs Elysees had a "fief reservé des Ebugors"[1]—*veuve* in the language of Sodom being the *maîtresse en titre,* the favorite youth.

At the decisive moment of monarchical decomposition Mirabeau[2] declares that pederasty was *reglementée.*

---

[1] The Boulgrin of Rabelais, which Urquhart renders Ingle for Boulgre, an "indorser," derived from the Bulgarus or Bulgarian, who gave to Italy the term bugiardo—liar. Bougre and Bougrerie date (Littré) from the thirteenth century. I cannot, however, but think that the trivial term gained strength in the sixteenth century when the manners of the Bugres or indigenous Brazilians were studied by Huguenot refugees in La France Antartique and several of these savages found their way to Europe. A grand Fête in Rouen on the entrance of Henri II. and Dame Katherine de Medicis (June 16, 1564) showed, as part of the pageant, three hundred men (including fifty "Bugres" or Tupis) with parroquets and other birds and beasts of the newly explored regions. The procession is given in the four-folding woodcut "Figure des Brésiliens" in Jean de Prest's Edition of 1551.

[2] Erotika Biblion chapt. Kadésch (pp. 93 et seq.) Edition de Bruxelles with notes by the Chevalier P. Pierrugues of Bordeaux, before noticed.

The Restoration and the Empire made the police more vigilant in matters of politics than of morals.[1] The favorite club, which had its *mot de passe,* was in the Rue Doyenne, old quarter St. Thomas des Louvre; and the house was a hôtel of the seventeenth century. Two street-doors, on the right for the male *gynæceum* and the left for the female, opened at 4 p.m. in winter and 8 p.m.

---

[1] Le goût des pédérastes, quoique moins en vogue que du temps de Henri III. (the French Heliogabalus), sous le règne desquel les hommes se provoquaient mutuellement sous les portiques du Louvre, fait des progrès considérables. On sait que cette ville (Paris) est un chef-d'œuvre de police; en conséquence, il y a des lieux publics autorisés à cet effet. Les jeunes gens qui se destinent à la profession, sont soigneusement enclassés; car les systèmes réglementaires s'étendent jusques-là. On les examine; ceux qui peuvent être agents et patients, qui sont beaux, vermeils, bien faits, potelés, sont réservés pour les grands seigneurs, ou se font payer très-cher par les évêques et les financiers. Ceux qui sont privés de leurs testicules, ou en termes de l'art (car notre langue est plus chaste qui nos mœurs), qui n'ont le *poids du tisserand,* mais qui donnent et reçoivent, forment la seconde classe; ils sont encore chers, parceque les femmes en usent tandis qu'ils servent aux hommes. Ceux qui ne sont plus susceptibles d'érection tant ils sont usés, quoiqu'ils aient tous ces organes nécessaires au plaisir, s'inscrivent comme *patiens purs,* et composent la troisième classe: mais celle qui préside à ces plaisirs, vérifie leur impuissance. Pour cet effet, on les place tout nus sur un matelas ouvert par la moitié inférieure; deux filles les caressent de leur mieux, pendant qu'une troisième frappe doucement avec

in summer. A decoy-lad, charmingly dressed in women's clothes, with big haunches and small waist, promenaded outside; and this continued till 1826 when the police put down the house.

Under Louis Philippe, the conquest of Algiers had evil results, according to the Marquis de Boissy. He complained *sans ambages* of *mœurs Arabes* in French regiments, and declared that the result of the African wars was an *éffrayable débordement pédérastique,* even as the *vérole* resulted from the Italian campaigns of that age of passion, the sixteenth century. From the military the *fléau* spread to civilian society and the Vice took such expansion and intensity that it may be said to have been democratized in cities and large towns; at least so we gather from the *Dossier des Agissements des Pédérastes.*

A general gathering of "La Sainte Congrégation des glorieux Pédérastes" was held in the old

---

des orties naissantes le siége des désirs vénériens. Après un quart d'heure de cet essai, on leur introduit dans l'anus un poivre long rouge qui cause une irritation considérable; on pose sur les échaubolures produites par les orties, de la moutarde fine de Caudebec, et l'on passe le *gland* au camphre. Ceux qui résistent à ces épreuves et ne donnent aucun signe d'érection, servent comme patiens à un tiers de paie seulement."

THE SOTADIC ZONE   95

Petite Rue des Marais where, after the theatre, many resorted under pretext of making water. They ranged themselves along the walls of a vast garden and exposed their *podices*: bourgeois, richards and nobles came with full purses, touched the part which most attracted them and were duly followed by it. At the Allée des Veuves the crowd was dangerous from 7 to 8 p.m.: no policeman or *ronde de nuit* dared venture in it; cords were stretched from tree to tree and armed guards drove away strangers amongst whom, they say, was once Victor Hugo. This nuisance was at length suppressed by the municipal administration.

The Empire did not improve morals. Balls of sodomites were held at No. 8 Place de la Madeleine where, on Jan. 2, 1864, some one hundred and fifty men met, all so well dressed as women that even the landlord did not recognize them. There was also a club for sotadic debauchery called the *Cent Gardes* and the *Dragons de l'Impératrice*.[1] They copied the imperial toilette

---

[1] Centuria Librorum Absconditorum (by Pisanus Fraxi) 4to, p. lx. and 593. London. Privately printed, 1879.

and kept it in the general wardrobe: hence "faire l'Impératrice" meant to be used carnally. The site, a splendid hotel in the Alleé des Veuves, was discovered by the Procureur-Général who registered all the names; but, as these belonged to not a few senators and dignitaries, the Emperor wisely quashed proceedings. The club was broken up on July 16, 1864.

During the same year La Petite Revue, edited by M. Loredan Larchy, son of the General, printed an article, "Les échappés de Sodome": it discusses the letter of M. Castagnary to the Progrès de Lyons and declares that the Vice had been adopted by *plusieurs corps de troupes*. For its latest developments as regards the *chantage* of the *tantes* (pathics), the reader will consult the last issues of Dr. Tardieu's well-known Etudes.[1]

---

[1] A friend learned in these matters supplies me with the following list of famous pederasts. Those who marvel at the wide diffusion of such erotic perversions, and its being affected by so many celebrities, will bear in mind that the greatest men have been some of the worst: Alexander of Macedon, Julius Cæsar and Napoleon Buonaparte held themselves high above the moral law which obliges commonplace humanity. All three are charged with the Vice. Of Kings we have Henri iii., Louis xiii. and xviii., Frederick ii. of Prussia, Peter the Great, William ii. of Holland and Charles ii. and iii. of Parma. We find also Shakespeare (i.,

He declares that the servant-class is most infected; and that the Vice is commonest between the age of fifteen and twenty-five.

The pederasty of the Arabian Nights may briefly be distributed into three categories. The first is the funny form, as the unseemly practical joke of masterful Queen Budúr (vol. iii. 300-306) and the not less hardy jest of the slave-princess Zumurrud (vol. iv. 226). The second is in the grimmest and most earnest phase of the perversion, for instance where Abu Nowas[1] de-

---

xv., Edit. François Hugo) and Molière, Theodorus Beza, Lully (the Composer), D'Assoucy, Count Zintzendorff, the Grand Condé, Marquis de Villette, Pierre Louis Farnèse, Duc de la Vallière, De Soleinne, Count D'Avaray, Saint Mégrin, D'Epernon, Admiral de la Susse, La Roche-Pouchin Rochfort, S. Louis, Henne (the Spiritualist), Comte Horace de Viel Castel, Lerminin, Fievée, Théodore Leclerc, Archi-Chancellier Cambacérès, Marquis de Custine, Sainte-Beuve and Count D'Orsay. For others refer to the three volumes of Pisanus Fraxi; Index Librorum Prohibitorum (London, 1877), Centuria Librorum Absconditorum (before alluded to) and Catena Librorum Tacendorum, London, 1885. The indices will supply the names.

[1] Of this peculiar character Ibn Khallikan remarks (ii. 43): "There were four poets whose works clearly contraried their character. Abu al-Atahíyah wrote pious poems himself being an atheist; Abú Hukayma's verses proved his impotence, yet he was more salacious than a he-goat; Mohammed ibn Házim praised

bauches the three youths (vol. v. 64-69); whilst in the third form it is wisely and learnedly discussed, to be severely blamed, by the Shaykhah or Reverend Woman (vol. v. 154).

To conclude this part of my subject, the *éclaircissement des obscénitês*. Many readers will regret the absence from the Arabian Nights of that modesty which distinguishes "Amadis de Gaul"; whose author when leaving a man and a maid together says: "And nothing shall be here related; for these and suchlike things which are conformable neither to good conscience nor nature, man ought in reason lightly to pass over, holding them in slight esteem as they deserve." Nor have we less respect for Palmerin of England who after a *risqué* scene declares: "Herein is no offence offered to the wise by wanton speeches, or encouragement to the loose by lascivious matter." But these are not oriental ideas and we must e'en take the Eastern as we find him. He still holds "Naturalia non sunt turpia," together with "Mundis omnia munda"; and, as Bacon assures

---

contentment, yet he was greedier than a dog; and Abú Nowás hymned the joys of sodomy, yet he was more passionate for women than a baboon."

us the mixture of a lie doth add to pleasure, so the Arab enjoys the startling and lively contrast of extreme virtue and horrible vice placed in juxtaposition.

Those who have read through the Arabian Nights will agree with me that the proportion of offensive matter bears a very small ratio to the mass of the work. In an age saturated with cant and hypocrisy, here and there a venal pen will mourn over their "Pornography," dwell upon the "Ethics of Dirt" and the "Garbage of the Brothel"; and will lament the "wanton dissemination (!) of ancient and filthy fiction." This self-constituted *Censor morum* reads Aristophanes and Plato, Horace and Virgil, perhaps even Martial and Petronius, because "veiled in the decent obscurity of a learned language"; he allows men *Latinè loqui*; but he is scandalized at stumbling-blocks much less important in plain English. To be consistent he must begin by bowdlerizing not only the classics, with which boys' and youths' minds and memories are soaked and saturated at schools and colleges, but also Boccaccio and Chaucer, Shakespeare and Rabelais; Burton, Sterne, Swift and a long list of works which are yearly reprinted and republished without a word of protest.

Lastly, why does not this inconsistent puritan purge the Old Testament of its allusions to human ordure and the pudenda; to carnal copulation and impudent whoredom, to adultery and fornication, to onanism, sodomy and bestiality? But this he will not do, the whited sepulchre! It appears to me that when I show to such men, so "respectable" and so impure, a landscape of magnificent prospects whose vistas are adorned with every charm of nature and art, they point their unclean noses at a little heap of muck here and there lying in a field-corner.

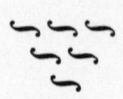

JOHN ADDINGTON SYMONDS ON THE SOTADIC ZONE

JOHN ADDINGTON SYMONDS
ON THE SOTADIC ZONE

∽

IN ENGLAND an Essay appended to the last volume of Sir Richard Burton's "Arabian Nights" made a considerable stir upon its first appearance. The author endeavored to co-ordinate a large amount of miscellaneous matter and to frame a general theory regarding the origin and prevalence of homosexual passions. His erudition, however, is incomplete, and though he possesses a copious store of anthropological details, he is not at the proper point of view for discussing the topic philosophically.

For example, he takes for granted that "Pederasty," as he calls it, is everywhere and always what the vulgar think it. He seems to have no notion of the complicated psychology of Urnings, revealed to us by their recently published confessions in French and German medical and legal works. Still, his views deserve consideration.

Burton regards the phenomenon as "geographical and climatic, not racial." He summarizes the result of his investigations in the following five conclusions:

"(1) There exists what I shall call a 'Sotadic Zone,' bounded westwards by the northern shores of the Mediterranean (N. lat. 43°) and by the southern (N. lat. 30°). Thus the depth would be 780 to 800 miles, including meridional France, the Iberian Peninsula, Italy and Greece, with the coast-regions of Africa from Morocco to Egypt.

"(2) Running eastward the Sotadic Zone narrows, embracing Asia Minor, Mesopotamia and Chaldæa, Afghanistan, Sind, the Punjab, and Kashmir.

"(3) In Indo-China the belt begins to broaden, enfolding China, Japan, and Turkistan.

"(4) It then embraces the South Sea Islands and the New World, where, at the time of its discovery, Sotadic love was, with some exceptions, an established racial institution.

"(5) Within the Sotadic Zone the vice is popular and endemic, held at the worst to be a mere peccadillo, whilst the races to the North and

ON THE SOTADIC ZONE   105

South of the limits here defined practise it only sporadically, amid the opprobrium of their fellows, who as a rule, are physically incapable of performing the operation, and look upon it with the liveliest disgust."

This is a curious and interesting generalization, though it does not account for what history has transmitted regarding the customs of the Kelts, Scythians, Bulgars, Tartars, Normans, and for the acknowledged leniency of modern Slavs to this form of vice.

Burton advances an explanation of its origin. "The only physical cause for the practice which suggests itself to me, and that must be owned to be purely conjectural, is that within the Sotadic Zone there is a blending of the masculine and feminine temperament, a crasis which elsewhere occurs only sporadically."

So far as it goes, this suggestion rests upon ground admitted to be empirically sound by medical writers and vehemently declared to be indisputable as a fact of physiology by Ulrichs. But Burton makes no effort to account for the occurrence of this crasis of masculine and feminine temperaments in the Sotadic Zone at large, and for its sporadic appearance in other regions. Would it not be more philosophical to conjecture that the crasis, if that exists at all, takes place universally; but that the consequences are only tolerated in certain parts of the globe, which he defines as the Sotadic Zone? Ancient Greece and Rome permitted them. Modern Greece and Italy have excluded them to the same extent as Northern European nations. North and South America, before the Conquest, saw no harm in them. Since its colonization by Europeans they have been discountenanced.

The phenomenon cannot therefore he regarded as specifically geographical and climatic. Besides, there is one fact mentioned by Burton which ought to make him doubt his geographical theory. He says that, after the conquest of Algiers, the French troops were infected to an enormous extent by the habits they had acquired there, and from them it spread so far and wide into civilian society that "the vice may be said to have been democratized in cities and large towns." This surely proves that north of the Sotadic Zone males are neither physically incapable of the acts involved in abnormal passion, nor gifted with an insuperable disgust for them. Law, and the public opinion generated by law and religious teaching, have been deterrent causes in those regions. The problem is therefore not geographical and climatic, but social.

Again, may it not be suggested that the absence of "the Vice" among the negroes and negroid races of South Africa, noticed by Burton, is due to their excellent customs of sexual initiation and education at the age of puberty—customs which it is the shame of modern civilization to have left unimitated?

However this may be, Burton regards the instinct as natural, not *contre nature,* and says that its patients "deserve, not prosecution but the pitiful care of the physician and the study of the psychologist."

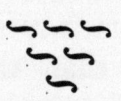